The New Corporate Finance, Capital Markets, and Valuation: An Introductory Text Workbook

J. Randall Woolridge
Gary Gray
Penn State University

KENDALL/HUNT PUBLISHING COMPANY
4050 Westmark Drive   Dubuque, Iowa 52002

The New Corporate Finance and Capital Markets

The New Corporate Finance and Capital Markets

This module provides a general overview of the role of corporate finance in organizations today. The objectives of the session include:

(1) An appreciation for the role of finance in businesses and the economy;

(2) The growing importance of capital markets in society, and the impact of this development on the role of finance in organizations;

(3) The responsibilities of the chief financial officer (CFO) in the new financial environment, and the skill set required of today's CFOs;

(4) The evolving role of the finance function in businesses; and

(5) The primary issues, basic tenets, financial toolbox of corporate finance

---

Financial Facts of the Day

The Largest Companies in the World

ale	Profit$

Corporate Finance

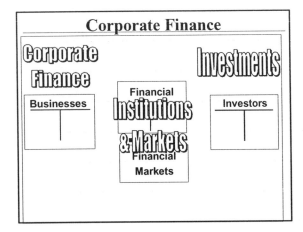

Financial Management – The Big Picture

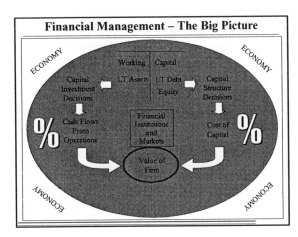

The New Corporate Finance and Capital Markets

1. The New Corporate Finance

2. The New Role of the CFO and the Evolving Finance Function

3. The Primary Issues in Corporate Finance

4. The Basic Tenets of Corporate Finance

The Finance Function

The Finance Function

Treasurer
Financial Planning
Capital Budgets
S-T and L-T Capital
Requirements
Cash Management
  and Working Capital

Controller
Financial Statements
  and Reports
Financial Systems
Operating Budgets
Audits
Taxes

The New Corporate Finance

1. The Finance Environment

2. Elements of the New
   Financial Environment

3. Advances in Finance

The Financial Environment

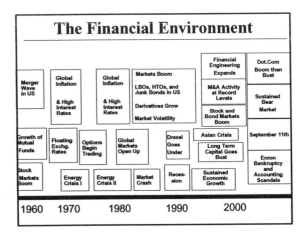

	Merger Wave in US	Global Inflation & High Interest Rates	Global Inflation & High Interest Rates	Markets Boom / LBOs, HTOs, and Junk Bonds in US / Derivatives Grow / Market Volatility	Financial Engineering Expands / M&A Activity at Record Levels / Stock and Bond Markets Boom	Dot.Com Boom then Bust / Sustained Bear Market
	Growth of Mutual Funds	Floating Exchg. Rates	Options Begin Trading	Global Markets Open Up	Drexel Goes Under	Asian Crisis / Long Term Capital Goes Bust	September 11th
	Stock Markets Boom	Energy Crisis I	Energy Crisis II	Market Crash	Recession	Sustained Economic Growth	Enron Bankruptcy and Accounting Scandals

1960   1970   1980   1990   2000

The Financial Environment

	Merger Wave in US	Global Inflation & High Interest Rates	Global Inflation & High Interest Rates	Markets Boom / LBOs, HTOs, and Junk Bonds in US / Derivatives Grow / Market Volatility	Financial Engineering Expands / M&A Activity at Record Levels / Stock and Bond Markets Boom	Dot.Com Boom then Bust / Sustained Bear Market
	Growth of Mutual Funds	Floating Exchg. Rates	Options Begin Trading	Global Markets Open Up	Drexel Goes Under	Asian Crisis / Long Term Capital Goes Bust	September 11th
	Stock Markets Boom	Energy Crisis I	Energy Crisis II	Market Crash	Recession	Sustained Economic Growth	Enron Bankruptcy and Accounting Scandals

1960   1970   1980   1990   2000
Theme: Growth and Volatility, with Bigger Role for Finance

The New Corporate Finance
Elements of the New Environment

Advances in Information, Systems, and Telecommunications Technologies

Growth in Trade and Direct Investment

Deregulation and Growth of Global Markets

Greater Economic Volatility and Risk

New Complex Financial Instruments

Institutionalization of Markets

New Markets and Financial Institutions

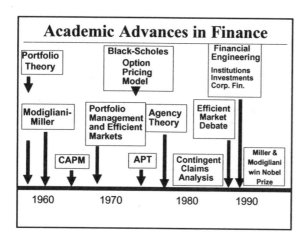

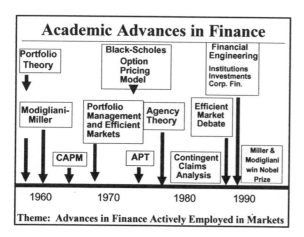

The CFO as Financial Engineer

Traditional Roles

■ <u>Controller Functions</u> – Planning and Control, Systems, Financial Statements and Reports, Taxes, Budgets

■ <u>Treasury Functions</u> – Cash and Working Capital Management, Capital Budgets, L-T Financial Planning

Expanded Roles

■<u>Corporate Strategist</u> – Assist in Strategy Formulation

■ <u>Financing and Capitalization</u> – Insure that Capital is Available to Fund Strategic Plan

■ <u>Risk Management</u> – Hedge Risks (Currency, Commodity, Financial) in Markets When Appropriate

■ <u>Growth and Acquisitions</u> – Provide for Growth Opportunities

Andy Bryant

Award For Finance Transformation In The Internet Era

Established A System Of Online Ordering And Procurement Of Supplies Over Internet

Implemented Electronic Payroll System

Development Of Improved Control Over Procurement And Inventory Has Been Greatest Financial Benefit To Intel

---

e Evolving Role of the Finance Functi

Command and Control	Competitive Team
Corporate Cops	Business Advocates
Financial Planning and Control	Understanding Business Units
Budgeting and Capital Allocation	Achieve Business Unit Targets
Control Financial Information	Share Financial Information
Not Accountable for Performance	Share Accountability for Performance

---

The Financial Environment

Master

Capital Markets

Slaves

The Focus on Capital Markets has Elevated Finance from Slave to Master – But Most People do not Understand How Capital Markets Work!

| 1960 | 1970 | 1980 | 1990 | 2000 |

Gamblers, Masters, and Slaves

The Primary Issues in Corporate Finance

1. What is a Firm Worth?
2. What Capital Structure Creates the Most Value?
3. Does the Cost of Capital for Firms Vary Between Countries, and if So, Why?
4. Does a Firm's Ownership Structure Affect the Answers to the First 3 Questions?

Strategic Financial Management

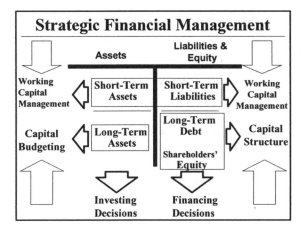

Strategic Financial Management

Assets	Liabilities & Equity
Current Assets Cash Accounts Receivable Inventories	**Current Liabilities** S-T Loans Accounts Payable

Working Capital Management
Managing Short Term Financial Position of the Firm

Strategic Financial Management

Assets	Liabilities & Equity
Long-Term Assets Property, Plant. & Equipment	

Capital Budgeting
Managing Investments in Long-Term Assets

Strategic Financial Management

Assets	Liabilities & Equity
	Long-Term Debt & Equity L-T Debt Shareholders Equity

Capital Structure
Managing Financing Mix Between Debt and Equity

The Basic Tenets of Corporate Finance

↗ **Creating Shareholder Value and Corporate Governance**

↗ **The Time Value of Money and Valuation**

↗ **Risk and Return**

↗ **Market Efficiency**

The Importance of Shareholder Value

- Management Has Fiduciary Responsibility to Act In Shareholder's Interests

- Shareholder Value Approach Favors Strategies That Enhance Company's Cash-Flow Generating Ability

- Creating Shareholder Value Minimizes Value Gaps

Time Value of Money

- A Dollar Today Is Worth More Than a Dollar Tomorrow

- How Much More Depends On Time Preference of Individual, Investment Opportunity, and Expected Inflation

- Understanding Time Value of Money Is Essential to Creating Shareholder Value

The Notion of a Risk Premium

Return (%)

Small Co. Common Stocks
Common Stocks
L-T Corp. Bonds
L-T Gov. Bonds
Treasury Bills

Risk Premium

Risk

Market Efficiency

- Composed of Well-Informed Individuals

- Trading Activities Cause Prices to Adjust Rapidly to Reflect All Relevant and Available Information

- New Information Arrive on Market In Random Order

- Therefore, Stock Prices Follow Random Walk

_____

_____

_____

_____

_____

_____

Financial Decisions and the Financial Tool Box

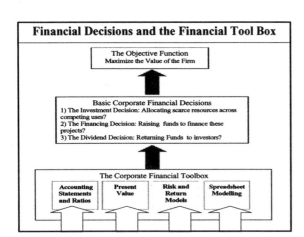

The Objective Function
Maximize the Value of the Firm

Basic Corporate Financial Decisions
1) The Investment Decision: Allocating scarce resources across competing uses?
2) The Financing Decision: Raising funds to finance these projects?
3) The Dividend Decision: Returning Funds to investors?

The Corporate Financial Toolbox

Accounting Statements and Ratios | Present Value | Risk and Return Models | Spreadsheet Modelling

_____

_____

_____

_____

_____

_____

New Corporate Finance and Capital Markets Key Learning Points

1. Corporate Finance, its Evolving Function, and the CFO

2. The New Environment of Corporate Finance

3. The Primary Issues in Corporate Finance

4. The Basic Tenets of Corporate Finance

5. The Financial Tool Box

_____

_____

_____

_____

_____

_____

Creating Shareholder Value and Corporate Governance

Creating Shareholder Value and Corporate Governance

Financial Facts of the Day

The Numbers You Have to Know

The DJIA
Price of Gold
30-Year Bond Yield
Yen/$ & Euro/$
NASDAQ

Creating Shareholder Value and Corporate Governance

This module explores the methods corporations employ to create shareholder value and the way in which these entities are governed. Objectives for this module include:

(1) Exploring the notion of creating shareholder value;
(2) Understanding the corporate organizational form as well as the "agency problem;"
(3) Discussing internal and external control mechanisms in corporations;
(4) Analyzing corporate governance in the 80's and 90's;
(5) Explore global models of corporate governance.

Creating Shareholder Value - What does it Mean?

Market Capitalization

- Market Cap – The Aggregate Market Value of a Company

    Market Cap =

    # of Shares * Price Per Share

- Why is it Important?

Hershey's

Statement of Corporate Philosophy

"As a Major Diversified Company, We are in Business to Make a Reasonable Profit, an Adequate Return on Our Investment, and to Enhance Our Stockholders' Investment"

Verizon

Verizon is Committed to Steady, Long-Term Growth in Shareholder Value

→ **Aggressive Top Line Growth**
→ **Productivity Improvement**
→ **Effective Investment Allocation**
→ **Balanced Funding Strategy**

Income Statement	Balance Sheet	
	Assets	Liabilities & Equity
Sales ➤ **Aggressive Top Line Growth** ➤ **Productivity Improvement** **Net Income**	**Make Good Investments** ➤ **Effective Investment Allocation**	**Effective Use of Debt And Equity Financing** ➤ **Balanced Funding Strategy**

veri_on

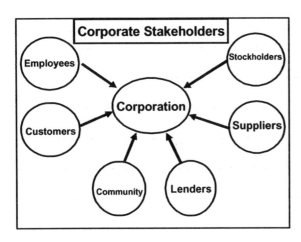

Corporate Stakeholders

Employees — Corporation — Stockholders — Customers — Suppliers — Community — Lenders

Stakeholders vs. Stockholders

What's the Big Difference?

Stockholders as the Residual Claimants:
An Income Statement View

Income Statement		Stakeholder Payments
Revenues	XXXX	
- Cost of Good Sold	XXX	Suppliers
= Gross Profit	XXX	
- Selling, General & Administrative Expenses	XXX	Employees
= Operating Profit	XXX	
- Interest Expense	XX	Lenders
= Profit Before Taxes	XX	
- Taxes	XX	Government
= Profit After Taxes	XX	

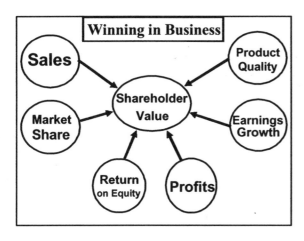

Winning in Business

Sales → Shareholder Value
Market Share → Shareholder Value
Return on Equity → Shareholder Value
Profits → Shareholder Value
Product Quality → Shareholder Value
Earnings Growth → Shareholder Value

Customer Satisfaction and Shareholder Value

Shareholder Value

Value Maximization

1   4   3   2

Customer Satisfaction →

Walt Disney Co.
Managing for Value

◆ **Resource Allocation to Areas of Competitive Strength**
- Theme Parks and Resorts, Movies and Television, Music, Imagineering, and New Entertainment Opportunities
- Selective Acquisitions in Related Areas
- Expand Consumer Products Base

◆ **Ownership and Financial Strategies**
- Use of Partnerships and Joint Ownerships
- Innovative Financing Strategies

The Coca-Cola Company
CEO Roberto Goizueta

> "We raise capital to make concentrate, and sell it at an operating profit. Then we pay the cost of capital. Shareholders pocket the difference."

Target Corp.

◆ **2nd Largest General Merchandise Retailer in US**
   - Operates 1,383 Stores in 47 States
   - Primary Growth in Target Store
   - Building 75 New Stores a Year (8-10%) in Less Penetrated Markets
   - Brand Building -- Innovative Merchandising and Compelling Value

◆ **Mid-1990s Restructuring**
   - Expanded Gross Margins from 25% to 31%
   - EPS Growth Rate Goal – 15%

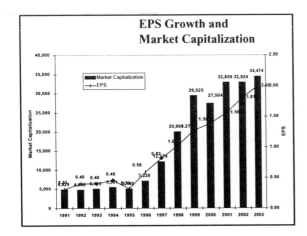

EPS Growth and
Market Capitalization

**Creating Shareholder
Value**

How does Management Create Shareholder Value?

Asset Management   **Liability Management**

Avenues of Shareholder Value Creation

Financial Management

Asset Management	Liability Management
Goal	**Goal**
To Allocate Capital to Investments Offering the Highest Risk-Adjusted Returns	To Minimize the Cost of Capital
To Minimize the Amount of Capital Required to Achieve the Company's Objective	o Financial Engineering - Debt/Equity Management - Financial Innovation - Strategic Risk Management
o Working Capital Management	To Enhance Performance
o Fixed Capital Management	o Ownership Structure

Business Organizational Forms

1. Sole Proprietorships
2. Partnerships
3. Corporations

Business Organization: The Sole Proprietorship

- **Sole Proprietorships: Businesses Owned By a <u>Single Individual</u>**

- **Inability to Raise Large Amounts of Money Limits Growth**

- **No Legal Distinction Between Business and Owner**

- **Enterprise Pays No Taxes: All Profits Accrue to Owner and Taxed as Personal Income**

Business Organization: Partnerships

- **Partnership**: Involve **Two or More Individuals Getting Together to Conduct Business**
- Owners Have **Unlimited Liability** For Business's Debt
- **Transfer of Ownership Is Difficult**: When One Partner Dies, Business Is Usually Dissolved
- **Inability to Raise Large Sums of Money**

Business Organization: The Corporate Entity

- **Corporation**: Distinct Legal Entities Separate From Owners and Managers
- **Advantages:**
  - Limited Liability
  - Ease of Ownership Transfer
  - Unlimited Life
  - Ability to Raise Capital
- Double Taxed
- Costly and Complex Process Involved to Start One

Form	Sole Proprietorship	Partnership	Corporation
Ease of Formation	Easy	More Difficult	Difficult – Separate Legal Entity
Tax	Profits Taxed as Income	Profits Taxed as Income	Double Taxed – Corp. & Individual
Ease of Transfer	Difficult	More Difficult	Easy
Liability	Liable for Liabilities	Liable for Liabilities	Limited Liability
Ability to Raise Capital	Difficult	Difficult	Relatively Easy

Corporate Governance

Corporate Governance

- ◆ **A Corporation is**
  - – Legal entity which serves as a nexus of contracts whereby individuals contract with each other in the name of the corporation
  - – is dynamic and not a creature of the state

- ◆ **Brief History**
  - – State chartering process
  - – Not always dominant organizational form
  - – Advantages of the corporate organizational form
  - – Limited liability
  - – Access to capital
  - – Liquidity for owners

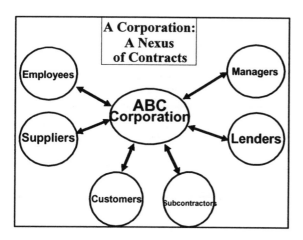

A Corporation: A Nexus of Contracts

What is Corporate Governance?

Corporation Governance

Corporate Governance:
The Agency Problem

◆ **Separation of Ownership and Control**
  – Berle & Means (1932) - *The Modern Corporation and Private Property*
  – Asset Ownership Versus Control

◆ **The Core Issue - The Agency Problem**
  – Managers are Agents of Stockholders
  – Managers May Act in Own Self Interest if Consequences are Not Severe Enough

---

The Agency Problem
Separation of Ownership and Control

Ownership

Stockholders

The Agency Problem

Control

Management

Corporate Control

Corporate Control Mechanisms Are Designed to Insure that Management Acts in Shareholder Interests

◆ **Internal Control Mechanisms**
 – Board of Directors
 – Audited Financial Statements
 – Stock Value–Based Compensation
 – Stock Ownership Interest

◆ **External Control Mechanisms**
 – Managerial Labor Market
 – Market for Corporate Control
 – Shareholder Activism

The US Board of Directors Model

Shareholders

▼ ▼ ▼

▼ ▼ ▼

Management

Corporate Takeovers in the 1980s: The Failure of Internal Control Mechanisms

◆ **Diffusion of Stock Ownership**
 – **Reduced Stockholder influence in Corporate Governance Issues**
 – **Costs of Monitoring Management Performance Too High**

◆ **Unfair Corporate Voting Procedures – Board Members & Management**
 – **Proxy Solicitation Procedures**
 – **Access to Stockholders**
 – **Nonconfidential voting**

◆ **Low Degree of Managerial Stock Ownership**

Managerial Defense Mechanisms

The White Knight: This occurs when the target company finds a friendly merger candidate. This strategy allows a merger to occur in a friendly manner and the current shareholders may also receive greater after-tax market value of securities if the deal is a "tax-free" exchange of stock;

The Pac-Man defense: Using this strategy, the target company employs a counter-takeover bid for the aggressor. The target company will announce that they are acquiring the aggressor and make the necessary advances to do so;

Greenmail: This is when the target company purchases the acquiror's shares at a premium over the market price;

Golden Parachutes: The golden parachute provides compensation to top-level executives in the event of a change of corporate control;

Self-Tender Offer: The target company agrees to purchase some of the current outstanding shares from its shareholders, usually at a price above what the acquiring company is offering;

Poison Pills: Poison pills are used to make a stock unappealing to others by making a takeover extremely expensive. They give current shareholders the right to purchase shares of the company at a bargain price, contingent on another firm acquiring control. This right dilutes the stock and makes a stock acquisition not conomically feasible; and

Crown Jewels: When threatened with a takeover attempt, the target company may sell off some of its major assets, or crown jewels.

Other People's Money

Questions

◆ Who are Gregory Peck and Danny Devito Talking to?

◆ Who has Replaced the Danny Devitos in the Public's Eye?

AMP

1. Who is the bidder, target, and white knight in this case study?
2. Why was AMP a takeover target?
3. What percentage premium (to the pre-offer price) was made by AlliedSignal?
4. How did AMP defend itself?
5. What role do the institutional investors play in the battle for AMP?
6. Why did Tyco's stock price fall at the announcement of its offer for AMP?
7. Who are the winners and losers in the battle for AMP?

AMP

1. Who is the bidder, target, and white knight in this case study?

    Bidder   ====

    Target   ====

    White Knight ====

AMP

2. Why was AMP a takeover target?

AMP Inc. EPS and Stock Price

AMP

3. What percentage premium (to the pre-offer price) was made by AlliedSignal?

AMP

4. How did AMP protect itself ?

_____

_____

_____

_____

_____

_____

_____

AMP

5. What role do the institutional investors play in the battle for AMP?

_____

_____

_____

_____

_____

_____

_____

AMP

6. Why did Tyco's stock price fall at the announcement of its offer for AMP?

AMP

7. Who are the winners an losers in the battle for AMP?

Winners   Losers

Corporate Governance
Since the 1980s

◆ **The Board's Role is Changing**
   - CEOs Fired for Poor Performance

◆ **Debate over Executive Compensation**
   - Management Pay Versus Performance
   - Issue of Management Stock Ownership

◆ **Institutional Investors are Becoming More Involved in Corporate Governance Issues**
   - Proxy Rules are Being Changed (Voting)
   - Shareholders Communications Permitted
   - The Demise of Managerial Defense Mechanisms (e.g., Poison Pills)
   - The Move to Shared Governance

Shareholder Activism and Stock Returns

The Council of Institutional Investors Annually Places Poorly Performing Companies on its 'Focus List'

Stock and Profit Performance for Laggard Companies Before and After Being Added to the CII Focus List

Cumulative Stock Performance

Legend: ▧ Focus List ■ Same Industry □ S&P 500

Y-axis: Cumulative Stock Performance — 0%, 20%, 40%, 60%, 80%, 100%

X-axis: Previous Four Years, Next Two Years

Return on Assets

Legend: ▧ Focus List ■ Same Industry □ S&P 500

Y-axis: Return on Assets — 0%, 5%, 10%, 15%, 20%

X-axis: Year Added, Three Years Later

Source: Opler and Sokobin

CII Core Board Policies to Maintain Independence

1. Directors should be elected annually with confidential voting;
2. At least two-thirds of the corporation's directors should be from outside the corporation to prevent biased opinions;
3. Shareholders should have adequate information regarding director backgrounds and status as independent or associated with the corporation;
4. All members of oversight committees should be independent directs to prevent biased opinions; and
5. A majority vote from common shareholders should be required to pass any major corporate decision.

Corporate Governance
Alternative Models

◆ **Anglo-American Model**
  - Minority Shareholders with Board
  - Problems Led to 1980s Takeovers

◆ **Japan-Germany Dedicated Capital Model**
  - Large Equity Holders Provide Oversight
  - Very Few Takeovers

◆ **Rest of World Majority Owner Model**
  - Majority Equity Owner Oversees Management

Corporate Governance

Alternative Models

Anglo-American Model

Characteristics:
Primarily Minority Shareholders
Board of Directors Elected to Represent Shareholders Interests
Fluid Capital Model – Capital Flows to Firms with Best Prospects
to Create Shareholder Value

Corporate Governance

Alternative Models

Japan		Germany
Kierstu	O	Hausbank

mitsubishi

Asahi Glass Co. Ltd	Mitsubishi Gas Chemical Company, Inc.	Mitsubishi Petroleum Co., Ltd
Asia Brewery Co. Ltd	Mitsubishi Heavy Industries, Ltd.	Mitsubishi Shindoh Co., Ltd.
Meiji Life Insurance Company	Mitsubishi Kakoki Kaisha, Ltd	Nikon Corporation
Mitsubishi Aluminum Company, Ltd	Mitsubishi Logistics Corporation	Nippon Mitsubishi Oil Corporation
Mitsubishi Cable Industries, Ltd	Mitsubishi Materials Corporation	Sanyo Tsusho Kabushiki Kaisha
Mitsubishi Chemical Corporation	Mitsubishi Motors Corporation	The Bank of Tokyo-Mitsubishi, Ltd.
Mitsubishi Constructions Co. Ltd	Mitsubishi Paper Mills Limited	The Mitsubishi Trust and Banking Corporation
Mitsubishi Corporation	Mitsubishi Plastics, Inc.	The Tokio Marine and Fire Insurance Co., Ltd.
Mitsubishi Electric Corporation	Mitsubishi Rayon Co., Ltd	Related Organizations / Others
Mitsubishi Estate Company, Limited	Mitsubishi Research Institute, Inc.	

Companies in Business Together that
Own Each Other's Common Stock

Deutsche Bank

DB is a Major Provider of Debt
And Equity Capital and is on
the Supervisory Board

DAIMLERCHRYSLER

Characteristics:
Dedicated Capital – Equity not Sold – Governance Issues

Corporate Governance

Alternative Models

Rest of World Majority Owner Model
Majority Equity Owner Oversees Management

Characteristics:
Company Managed According to the Interests
Of the Majority Owner

The Crisis in Corporate Governance

- Executive Compensation
- The Board of Directors
- Accounting and Auditing
- Wall Street Analysts
- The Justice Department and the SEC:
    Enforcement and
      Transparency
- Leadership

The Crisis in Corporate Governance
Executive Compensation

The Crisis in Corporate Governance
Auditing and Accounting

Global Crossing

Conflicts of Interest

Joseph Perrone, Executive VP of finance at Global Crossing (GC), previously headed the Arthur Anderson team responsible for auditing GC's books

At GC, Perrone was in charge of overseeing the way that GC booked revenue from network capacity swaps

Those accounting methods are under investigation by the SEC and FBI

Source: Jubak, Jim. "8 Companies Whose Board Need a Scare" MSN/Money. 2 April 2002

The Crisis in Corporate Governance
The Board of Directors

Adelphia Communications

Adelphia

The Board of Directors

Where's the Board of Directors?

Guaranteed loans of $2.3 Billion to Rigas family who founded and own most of Adelphia

Adelphia CFO said that the loan was secured by assets that would normally be able to secure no more than $700 Million

Debt, which Adelphia was liable for, did not appear on balance sheet

CFO: Timothy Rigas, son of then CEO John Rigas

Source: Jubak, Jim. "8 Companies Whose Board Need a Scare" MSN/Money. 2 April 2002

The Crisis in Corporate Governance
Wall Street Analysts

The Crisis in Corporate Governance
The Justice Department
& the SEC

Al Dunlap & Sunbeam

The notorious Al "Chainsaw" Dunlap, accused of zealously fabricating Sunbeam's financial statements when he was chief executive, is facing only civil, not criminal, charges. The SEC charged that Dunlap and his minions made use of every accounting fraud in the book, from "channel stuffing" to "cookie jar reserves." The case is now in the discovery phase of trial and likely to be settled; he has denied wrongdoing. (Earlier Chainsaw rid himself of a class-action shareholder suit for $15 million, without admitting culpability.) Whatever the current trial's outcome, Dunlap will still come out well ahead. Sunbeam, now under bankruptcy protection, gave him $12.7 million in stock and salary during 1998 alone. And if worse comes to worst, he can always tap the stash he got from the sale of the disemboweled Scott Paper to Kimberly-Clark, which by Dunlap's own estimate netted him a $100 million bonanza.

Sunbeam investors, naturally, didn't fare as well. When the fraud was discovered internally, the company was forced to restate its earnings, slashing half the reported profits from fiscal 1997. After that embarrassment, Sunbeam shares fell from $52 to $7 in just six months--a loss of $3.8 billion in market cap. Sound familiar?

The auditor in that case, you'll recall, was Arthur Andersen, which paid $110 million to settle a civil action. According to an SEC release in May, an Andersen partner authorized unqualified audit opinions even though "he was aware of many of the company's accounting improprieties and disclosure failures." The opinions were false and misleading. But nobody is going to jail.

At Waste Management, yet another Andersen client, income reported over six years was overstated by $1.4 billion. Andersen coughed up $220 million to shareholders to wipe its hands clean. The auditor, agreeing to the SEC's first antifraud injunction against a major firm in more than 20 years, also paid a $7 million fine to close the complaint. Three partners were assessed fines, ranging from $30,000 to $50,000, as well.

33

Sarbanes-Oxley Act of 2002

◆ CEOs Must Sign Off on Financial Statements

◆ Audit Committees Must Be Composed of Outside Directors

◆ Companies Cannot Make Loans to Directors

Financial Ethics

Finally, a price must be exacted for failure to do the right thing. "We had Sunbeam, Waste Management (WMI), and Cendant--and I don't think anybody has gone to jail yet, and I don't know why," says Philip B. Livingston, president of Financial Executives International, a professional group of finance managers. "When the SEC and the Justice Dept. get their act together and start sending some CFOs and CEOs to jail, you'll see a real wake-up call."

Creating Shareholder Value and Corporate Governance

Key Learning Points

1. Creating Shareholder Value

2. Avenues of Value Creation

3. Corporate Form of Organization

4. The Agency Problem and Corporate Control

5. Governance in the 80's and 90's

6. Global Corporate Governance

7. The Crisis in Corporate Governance

7. Gekko, Devito, and AMP

34

Strategic Financial Management

Strategic Financial Management

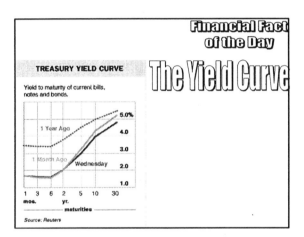

Financial Fact of the Day

The Yield Curve

TREASURY YIELD CURVE

Yield to maturity of current bills, notes and bonds.

5.0%
4.0
3.0
2.0
1.0

1 Year Ago
1 Month Ago   Wednesday

1 3 6   2   5 10   30
mos.   yr.
········· maturities ·········

Source: Reuters

Strategic Financial Management

This module covers the primary areas of strategic financial management. The objectives of the session include:

(1) Illustrating short-term financial strategy in the the form of working capital management;

(2) Assessing capital budgeting in the context of a firm;

(3) Evaluating the role of capital structure and dividend policy in long-term financial strategy.

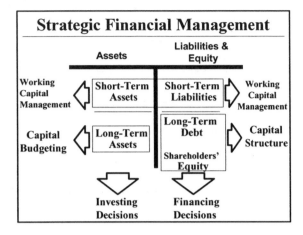

Strategic Financial Management

	Assets		Liabilities & Equity	
Working Capital Management	Short-Term Assets		Short-Term Liabilities	Working Capital Management
Capital Budgeting	Long-Term Assets		Long-Term Debt / Shareholders' Equity	Capital Structure
	Investing Decisions		Financing Decisions	

Strategic Financial Management

Assets	Liabilities & Equity
Current Assets Cash Accounts Receivable Inventories	**Current Liabilities** S-T Loans Accounts Payable

Working Capital Management
Managing Short Term Financial Position of the Firm

Working Capital Management

1. Old Paradigm/New Paradigm

2. The Costs of Holding Current Assets

3. The Short-Term Operating Cycle and the Cash Conversion Cycle

4. Financing Short-Term Assets

Working Capital Management

→ **Old Paradigm**
  - Working Capital
    is Good (liquidity)
  - Measure:
    Current Ratio of 2.0

→ **New Paradigm**
  - Working Capital is Bad
  - Reflects Poor Planning
  - Use of Funds
  - Measure: W/C / Sales

The Costs of Holding Current Assets

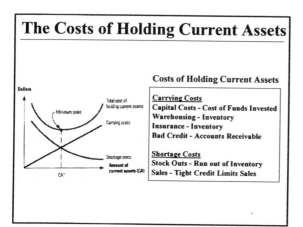

Costs of Holding Current Assets

Carrying Costs
Capital Costs - Cost of Funds Invested
Warehousing - Inventory
Insurance - Inventory
Bad Credit - Accounts Receivable

Shortage Costs
Stock Outs - Run out of Inventory
Sales - Tight Credit Limits Sales

The Costs of Maintaining Inventory

Inventory Costs as a Percent of Inventory

Warehousing Costs	
Space	
Utilities	
Taxes	
Equipment	0.60
People	
Fringe Benefits	
Spoilage and Obsolescence	0.30
Computer and Financial Systems to Monitor Inventories	0.20
Insurance	0.05
Cost of Capital	1.00
Total Cost	**2.15**

Biggest Costs:
Warehousing & Capital

Old Paradigm:
Excess Inventory adds
Value to Customers

New Paradigm:
Reduce Inventory by
Changing Processes and
Working with Suppliers

Short-Term Operating Cycle

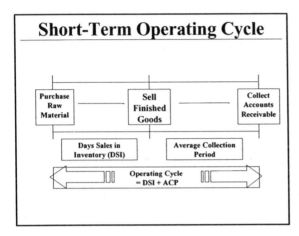

Purchasing and Accounts Payable

➜ **Old Paradigm**
- The Supplier is an Adversary
- Key Issue: Lower Prices

➜ **New Paradigm**
- Timeliness of Delivery May be More Important Than Price
- Good Purchasing Includes Terms, Quality, and Delivery
- The Cost of not Taking Discounts is Prohibitive

Working Capital Management

Assets	Liabilities
Cash Marketable Securities	Bank Loans

Accounts Receivable
Credit Policy
  - A/R Turn - ACP (Days Sales Outstanding)
 	
Inventories
Inventory Policy
  - Inv Turn - (Days in Inventory)
	Accounts Payable
	Payables Policy
	  - Payables Turn - (Days Payables Outstanding)

	Accrued Expenses
Total Current Assets	Total Current Liabilities

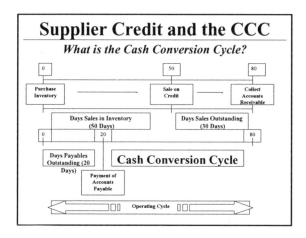

Supplier Credit and the CCC

What is the Cash Conversion Cycle?

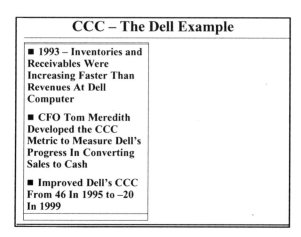

CCC – The Dell Example

■ 1993 – Inventories and Receivables Were Increasing Faster Than Revenues At Dell Computer

■ CFO Tom Meredith Developed the CCC Metric to Measure Dell's Progress In Converting Sales to Cash

■ Improved Dell's CCC From 46 In 1995 to –20 In 1999

Calculating the CCC

CCC	=	DSO	+	DSI	-	DPO

■ CCC = Cash Conversion Cycle

■ DSO = Days Sales Outstanding or Average Collection Period

■ DSI = Days Sales In Inventory

■ DPO = Days Payables Outstanding or Average Payables Period

CASH CONVERSION CYCLE

Calculating the CCC

■ Days Sales Outstanding or Average Collection Period:

$$DSO = \frac{Accounts\ Receivables}{Sales/365}$$

■ Days Sales In Inventory:

$$DSI = \frac{Inventory}{COGS/365} = \frac{365}{Inventory\ Turnover}$$

■ Days Payables Outstanding or Average Payables Period:

$$DPO = \frac{Accounts\ Payable}{COGS/365}$$

Strategic Financial Management

Cash Conversion Cycle	=	Days Sales Outstanding	+	Days Sales in Inventory	−	Days Payables Outstanding
CCC	=	DSO	+	DSI	−	DPO

Metric	1995	1997	1999
Days Sales Outstanding	42	37	38
Days Sales in Inventory	37	13	6
Days Payables Outstanding	33	54	64
Cash Conversion Cycle	46	-5	-20

Improving the Firm's CCC

■ Firms Can Do the Following to Improve Their Cash Conversion Cycle:

■ Expedite Collections

■ Increase Inventory Turnover (E.g., JIT Technique)

■ Lengthen Payables Period

Strategic Financial Management

Cash Conversion Cycle	=	Days Sales Outstanding	+	Days Sales in Inventory	-	Days Payables Outstanding
CCC	=	DSO	+	DSI	-	DPO

Target   WalMart

Financing Short-Term Assets

The Hedged Approach

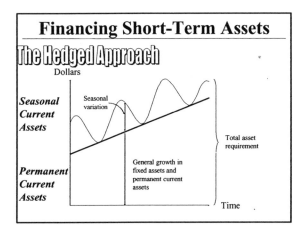

Capital Budgeting

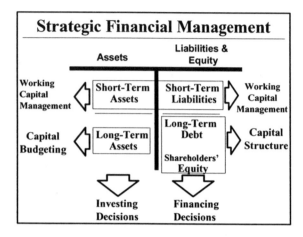

Capital Budgeting
Definition

The Capital Allocation Process Involves Current Outlays of Funds in Anticipation of Generating Future Cash Flows

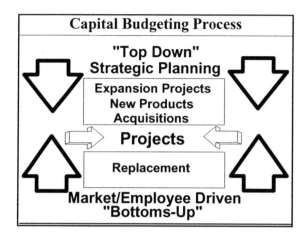

Capital Budgeting Process

"Top Down"
Strategic Planning

Expansion Projects
New Products
Acquisitions

Projects

Replacement

Market/Employee Driven
"Bottoms-Up"

◆ **Planning and Budgeting**
  - Identifying Potential
  Projects in the Strategic
  Planning Process

◆ **Evaluation**
  - Projecting Cash Flows and
  Applying Capital
  Budgeting Techniques

◆ **Post-Completion Reviews**
  - Compare Actual Versus
  Projected Results

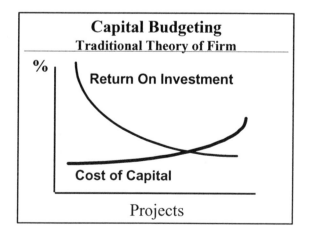

Capital Budgeting
Traditional Theory of Firm

%

Return On Investment

Cost of Capital

Projects

Capital Investment and Market Values
Investment Decisions and Stock Prices

Market Adjusted Returns

Days Around Investment Announcement

Capital Budgeting

→ **Types of Corporate Investment Decisions**
  - **Replacement**
  - **Expansion**

Capital Budgeting
Good Investments?

→ Microsoft Spent over $500 M Developing Windows 95/98

→ Boeing has Spent over $ 5 B Developing the 777

→ The Alaskian Pipeline Cost over $15 B

→ Disney Spent $50M Making *The Lion King*

Capital Budgeting
Bad Investments?

→ GM Invested Invested Over $101 Billion During the 1980s on Company Infrastructure

→ IBM Spent over $25 B on R&D During the 1985-1990 Period

→ RJR-Nabisco Spent $100 M on a Smokeless Cigarette Which was Never Marketed

→ EuroDisney Cost Over $4 B

Categories of Investments
Expansion

Motorola

The Iridium Project

Motorola, Along With Over 50 Global Partners, Spent Over $5B to Launch and Deploy 66 Satelites to Provide Cellular Communications Worldwide

---

Capital Budgeting

→ The Returns of a College Education

Capital Budgeting
The Returns of a College Education

➔ <u>Cost</u>
 − Avg. Cost − $22,000/Year

➔ <u>Salary Differentials</u>
 − College Grads Earn 89% More Than Non-Grads, Up From 49% More in 1979

➔ <u>Return</u>
 − Assuming 75% of Difference Due to Education, You Earn an 11% Return

Business Week, March 18, 1996

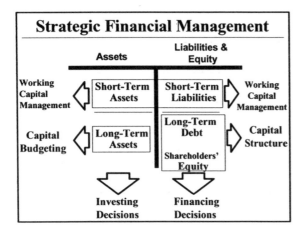

Strategic Financial Management

Assets | Liabilities & Equity

Working Capital Management — Short-Term Assets | Short-Term Liabilities — Working Capital Management

Capital Budgeting — Long-Term Assets | Long-Term Debt / Shareholders' Equity — Capital Structure

Investing Decisions | Financing Decisions

Strategic Financial Management

Assets | Liabilities & Equity

<u>Long-Term Debt & Equity</u>
L-T Debt
Shareholders
Equity

Capital Structure
Managing Financing Mix Between Debt and Equity

Capital Structure and Firm Valuation

→ Companies Need Capital to Grow

→ For a Typical Firm, 70% is Generated Internally from Operations

→ The Remainder Must be Raised from the Markets

→ Key Issue:
   Should it be Debt or Equity

Using Debt to Raise Capital

◆ Advantages
   - Interest is Tax Deductible

◆ Disadvantages
   - Incurr a Fixed Financing Obligation in the Form of Interest and Principle Payments Which can Lead to Financial Distress

Using Common Stock to Raise Capital

◆ Advantages
   - No Fixed Financing Obligation

◆ Disadvantages
   - Dilutes Ownership Interests
   - Higher Cost Than Debt

Capital Structure Policies

	Debt %	Equity %	# Times Interest Earned	Financial Strength	Sales Growth	Stock Risk 1-Low--5-High
Microsoft	0	100	nmf	A++	12%	4
Intel	3	97	30X	A++	6%	5
Coca-Cola	20	80	21X	A++	6%	2
Merck	22	78	22X	A++	12%	3
WalMart	32	68	10X	A++	12%	3
The Walt Disney Company	35	65	6X	A	5%	4
McDonald's	47	53	7X	A++	5%	3
Consolidated Edison	50	50	4X	A++	2%	1
Hilton Hotels	72	28	2X	C++	2%	4
AMR Corp.	83	17	2X	C	NMF	5
Nextel Communications	86	14	2X	C+	6%	5

Data Source: *Value Line Investment Survey*.

Capital Structure and Firm Valuation

♦ **Capital Structure Ratios of US Industry**
 - **High Degrees of Leverage Public Utilities, Publishing, Broadcasting, Real Estate, Transportation**
 - **Low Degrees of Leverage Computer Software, Drugs**

♦ **Capital Structure Policies**

Capital Structure and Firm Valuation
The Capital Structure Puzzle

♦ **Does An Optimal Capital Structure Exist?**
 - **Can the Use of Debt Financing Increase Firm Value?**

♦ **The Static Trade-Off Theory**
 - **Trade–Off Between Tax Savings and Financial Distress Costs of Debt**

Financing Pecking Order

- Pecking Order: Internal Financing, Debt and Equity

- Preference For Internal Financing

- Insulation From Capital Markets

- Reduces Transaction Costs and Problems Associated With Asymmetric Information

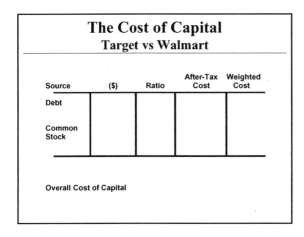

Internal Financing

Debt

Equity

The Cost of Capital
Target vs Walmart

Source	($)	Ratio	After-Tax Cost	Weighted Cost
Debt				
Common Stock				

Overall Cost of Capital

The Cost of Capital
Target vs Walmart

Source	($)	Ratio	After-Tax Cost	Weighted Cost
Debt				
Common Stock				

Overall Cost of Capital

Other Factors Influencing Financial Structure

- **Need to Preserve Financial Flexibility Limit Use of Debt**

- **With More Debt, Firms Become Easy Prey to Competitors**

- **Need For Financial Reserves Valuable to Firms With Limited Access to Financial Markets**

- **Firms With Growth Options Should Maintain Large Financial Reserves**

Capital Structure and Firm Valuation
The Determinants of Corporate Debt Levels

◆ **The Tax–Shield Effect of Interest Payments**

◆ **The Relative Degree of Business Risk**
  - **The Probability and Cost of Incurring Financial Distress**

◆ **The Nature of a Firm's Assets and Value**
  - **Tangible Assets and Value**
  - **Intangible Assets and Value**

◆ **Financial Slack**
  - **Investment Opportunities**
  - **Growth**

◆ **The Ownership Structure of the Firm**

Dividend Policy and Firm Valuation

Dividend Changes and Stock Prices
Dividend Increases and Decreases

Dividend Increases

Dividend Decreases

Source: J. Randall Wooldridge, Dividend Changes and Stock Returns"

Dividend Payout Policies

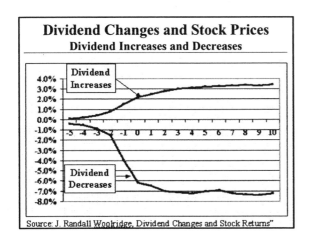

	Stock Price	2003 Dividend	Dividend Yield	2003 Earnings	Dividend Payout Ratio	Projected Dividend Growth
Microsoft	$ 25	$ 0.08	0.3%	$ 0.95	8.4%	25%
Intel	$ 16	$ 0.10	0.6%	$ 0.60	16.7%	10%
Coca-Cola	$ 40	$ 0.84	2.1%	$ 1.92	43.8%	8%
Merck	$ 60	$ 1.46	2.4%	$ 3.45	42.3%	8%
WalMart	$ 48	$ 0.32	0.7%	$ 2.05	15.6%	12%
The Walt Disney Company	$ 16	$ 0.21	1.3%	$ 0.70	30.0%	0%
McDonald's	$ 13	$ 0.26	2.0%	$ 1.45	17.9%	5%
Consolidated Edison	$ 40	$ 2.36	5.9%	$ 3.10	76.1%	1%
Hilton Hotels	$ 12	$ 0.08	0.7%	$ 0.45	17.8%	0%
AMR Corp.	$ 2	$ -	NMF	$ (7.50)	0%	Nil
Nextel Communications	$ 12	$ -	NMF	$ 0.70	0%	Nil

Data Source: *Value Line Investment Survey*.

Dividend Payout Policies

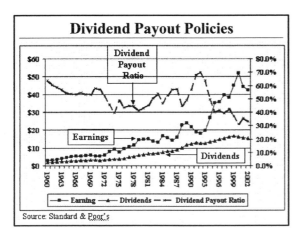

Dividend Payout Ratio

Earnings

Dividends

Earning — Dividends — Dividend Payout Ratio

Source: Standard & Poor's

- → When Will Microsoft Pay a Cash Dividend?

- → Traditionally Dividends have been Heresy to Tech Highfliers

- → Microsoft has $36B in Cash on its Balance Sheet - More Than an Other US Company

- → Microsoft Generates $1 B in Cash Each Month

- → Growth is Slowing, as is the Need for Cash for Acquisitions

- → The Company does Spend $6B on Stock Buybacks per Year

Dividend Policy and Firm Value
Summary Points

- → A Firm's Dividend Policy is Primarily a Function of It's Investment Opportunities

- → Announcements of Dividend Changes are Usually Accompanied with Like Changes in Stock Prices

- → Stock Prices React to Dividend Change Announcements due to the Information in the Announcements, Not Due to the Dividend Itself

Financial Statements, Analysis and Financial Ethics

Financial Statements

Financial Statements

This module introduces the main financial statements
and ratios used by firms to measure and monitor firm
performance. Objectives include:

(1) An <u>overview of financial accounting</u> and financial
statements;
(2) An understanding of <u>basic accounting conventions</u> and
how they affect financial statements;
(3) The <u>three basic financial statements</u> and how they are
interelated; and
(4) A review of the financial statements of Target Corp.

Financial Decisions and the Financial Tool Box

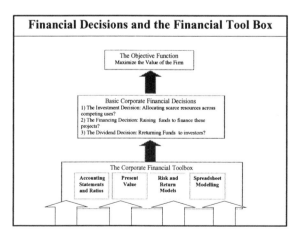

Which is the Biggest Public Accounting Firm?

ARTHUR ANDERSEN

Deloitte & Touche LLP

ERNST & YOUNG
FROM THOUGHT TO FINISH.™

KPMG

PRICEWATERHOUSECOOPERS

Major Internal and External Stakeholder Groups

Government
Investors
Community
Analysts
Board of Directors
Management
Employees
Suppliers
Customers
Employees
Creditors

What is GAAP?

GAAP is an acronym that stands for Generally Accepted Accounting Principles. Members of the accounting profession, through associations and individual input into the process, have over the years worked to establish accounting principles accepted by both the accounting profession and the public that relies on the profession's expertise.

Financial Reporting

The **balance sheet** reports, as of a certain point in time, the resources of a company (the assets), the company's obligations (the liabilities), and the equity of the owners.	The **income statement** reports, for a certain interval, the net assets generated through business operations (revenues), the net assets consumed (the expenses), and the net income.	The **statement of cash flows** reports, for a certain interval, the amount of cash generated and consumed by a company through operating, financing, and investing activities.

Financial Reporting

Accounting estimates and judgments are outlined in the **notes to financial statements.**

Basic Accounting Concepts
The Uses of Financial Statements

- ◆ **Administrative Control**

- ◆ **Resource Allocation**

- ◆ **Management Stewardship**

Evolution of Approach to Financial Statements

- After Great Depression: Focus on Balance Sheet
- Investors Avoided Stocks Trading Above Book Value
- Cautious With Leverage
- Today: Market Places Value on Both Tangible and Intangibles Assets
- Today, DJIA Trades At 8x Book Value

Basic Accounting Concepts
Financial Statement Terminology

- Sales
  - Revenues

- Cost of Goods Sold
  - Cost of Sales (Revenues)

- Net Earnings
  - Net Profits
  - Net Income

- Shareholders' Equity
  - Net Worth
  - Common Equity
  - Stockholders' Equity

- Fixed Assets
  - Property, Plant and Equipment

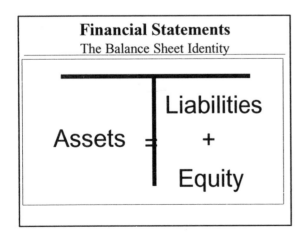

Financial Statements
The Balance Sheet Identity

$$Assets = Liabilities + Equity$$

Financial Statements
The Balance Sheet Identity

Assets = Liabilities + Equity

- Current Assets
- Current Liabilities
- Fixed Assets
  - o Tangible
  - o Intangible
- Long-Term Debt
- Common Equity

Market vs. Book Value

Balance Sheet

(in millions of USD)	12 Months ending January 31,		
	2001	**2002**	**2003**
Assets			
Cash & Cash Equivalents	356	499	758
Accounts & Notes Receivable	1,941	3,831	5,565
Inventories	4,248	4,449	4,760
Other Current Assets	759	869	852
Total Current Assets	7,304	9,648	11,935
Fixed Assets, Net	11,418	13,533	15,307
Other assets	768	973	1,361
Total Assets	19,490	24,154	28,603
Liabilities			
Accounts Payable	3,576	4,160	4,684
Short-Term Debt	857	905	975
Other Short-Term Liabilities	1,868	1,989	1,864
Total Current Liabilities	6,301	7,054	7,523
Long-Term Debt	5,634	8,088	10,186
Other Long-Term Liabilities	1,036	1,152	1,451
Total Liabilities	12,971	16,294	19,160
Stockholders' Equity			
Capital Stock & APIC	977	1,173	1,336
Retained Earnings	5,542	6,687	8,107
Total Stockholders' Equity	6,519	7,860	9,443

Notes to Financial Statements

Accounts Receivable

Through our special purpose subsidiary, Target Receivables Corporation (TRC), we transfer, on an ongoing basis, substantially all of our receivables to the Target Credit Card Master Trust (the Trust) in return for certificates representing undivided interests in the Trust's assets. TRC owns the undivided interest in the Trust's assets.

Inventory (millions)	2001	2002
Target	$3,348	$3,700
Mervyn's	822	861
Marshall Field's	348	388
Other	250	301
Total Inventory	$4,440	$4,248

Owned and Leased Store Locations

At year-end, owned, leased and "combined" (combination owned/ leased) store locations by operating segment were as follows:

	Owned	Leased	Combined	Total
Target	822	52	188	1,062
Mervyn's	159	8	47	264
Marshall Field's	51	12	1	64
Total	1,062	186	178	1,381

Long-term Debt and Notes Payable (millions)	February 2, 2002 Rate*	Balance	February 3, 2001 Rate*	Balance
Notes payable	1.8%	$ 100	5.8%	$ 608
Notes and debentures:				
Due 2001-2005	6.3	2,010	7.4	2,188
Due 2006-2010	6.4	2,980	7.1	1,808
Due 2011-2015	6.9	186	8.6	174
Due 2016-2020	9.7	136	9.7	135
Due 2021-2025	8.3	616	8.3	616
Due 2026-2030	6.7	400	6.7	403
Due 2031-2037	7.0	700		—
Total notes payable, notes and debentures	6.3%	$8,940	7.2%	$6,335
Capital lease obligations		153		156
Less: current portion		(906)		(857)
Long-term debt and notes payable		$8,088		$5,634

Basic Accounting Concepts
Income Statement

Fundamental Concepts

◆ GAAP and the Income Statement

◆ Non-Cash Items

◆ Time and Costs

Financial Statements
The Income Statement

◆ **GAAP and the Income Statement**
  - Revenue - Expenses = Net Income
  - GAAP - Matching of Costs with Revenues

◆ **Non-Cash Items**
  - Especially Depreciation
  - Matching of Costs With Revenues

◆ **Time and Costs**
  - Fixed vs. Variable Costs
  - Product Costs - (RM, DL, and OH)
  - Period Costs (SGA)

Basic Accounting Concepts
What Do Earnings Measure?

Fundamental Concepts

◆ **Realization Principle** Revenue is Recognized When a Good or Service is Provided

◆ **Matching Principle** Expenses Incurred in Providing a Good or Service are Recognized in the Period That the Sale is Made

Income Statement

Sales	xxxx
- Cost of Good Sold	xxx
= Gross Income (Profit)	xxx
-SG&A Expenses	xx
-R&D Expense	xx
-Depreciation	xx
=Operating Income (Profit)	xx
-Interest Expense	xx
=Profit Before Taxes	xx
-Taxes	xx
=Net Income (Profit)	xx

(in millions of USD)	12 Months ending January 31,		
	2001	2002	2003
Sales	36,903	39,888	43,917
COGS	25,295	27,246	29,260
Gross Profit	11,608	12,642	14,657
SG&A	9,130	9,962	11,393
EBIT	2,478	2,680	3,264
Interest Expense	425	464	588
Non-Operating Income/Loss, Ne	0	0	0
EBT	2,053	2,216	2,676
Income Tax Expense	789	842	1,022
Income from Continuing Operatio	1,264	1,374	1,654
EO Items & Discontinued Operati	0	-6	0
Net Income	1,264	1,368	1,654

Notes to Financial Statements

Significant Accounting Policies

Revenues Revenue from retail sales is recognized at the time of sale. Commissions earned on sales generated by leased departments are included within sales. Net credit revenues are comprised of finance charges and late fees on credit sales and third-party merchant fees earned from the use of our Target Visa credit card.

Cost of sales Cost of sales includes the cost of merchandise sold calculated utilizing the retail inventory accounting method. It includes estimates of shortage that are adjusted upon physical inventory counts in subsequent periods and estimates of amounts due from vendors for certain merchandise allowances and rebates. These estimates are consistent with our historical experience. It also includes a LIFO provision that is calculated based on inventory levels, markup rates and internally generated retail price indices.

Selling, general and administrative expense Selling, general and administrative expense includes expenses related to store operation, distribution, advertisement and administration. It also includes estimates for the present value cost of workers' compensation and general liability claims.

Financial Statements
Common Size Financial Statements

◆ **Common Size Income Statement**
  - All Accounts Expressed as a Percent of Net Sales

◆ **Common Size Balance Sheet**
  - All Asset Accounts Expressed as a Percent of Total Assets
  - All Liability/Equity Accounts Exressed as a Percent of Total Liabilities + Equity

---

(in millions of USD)	12 Months ending January 31,		
	2001	2002	2003
Assets			
Cash & Cash Equivalents	1.8%	2.1%	2.7%
Accounts & Notes Receivable	10.8%	15.9%	19.5%
Inventories	21.0%	18.4%	16.6%
Other Current Assets	3.9%	3.6%	3.0%
Total Current Assets	37.5%	39.9%	41.7%
Fixed Assets, Net	58.6%	56.0%	53.6%
Other assets	3.9%	4.0%	4.8%
Total Assets	100.0%	100.0%	100.0%
Liabilities			
Accounts Payable	18.3%	17.2%	16.4%
Short-Term Debt	4.4%	3.7%	3.4%
Other Short-Term Liabilities	9.6%	8.2%	6.5%
Total Current Liabilities	32.3%	29.2%	26.3%
Long-Term Debt	28.9%	33.5%	36.6%
Other Long-Term Liabilities	5.3%	4.8%	5.1%
Total Liabilities	66.6%	67.5%	67.0%
Stockholders' Equity			
Capital Stock & APIC	5.0%	4.9%	4.7%
Retained Earnings	28.4%	27.7%	28.3%
Total Stockholders' Equity	33.4%	32.5%	33.0%

(in millions of USD)	12 Months ending January 31,		
	2001	2002	2003
Sales	100.0%	100.0%	100.0%
COGS	68.5%	68.3%	66.6%
Gross Profit	31.5%	31.7%	33.4%
SG&A	24.7%	25.0%	25.9%
EBIT	6.7%	6.7%	7.4%
Interest Expense	1.2%	1.2%	1.3%
Non-Operating Income/Loss, Net	0.0%	0.0%	0.0%
EBT	5.6%	5.6%	6.1%
Income Tax Expense	2.1%	2.1%	2.3%
Income from Continuing Operations	3.4%	3.4%	3.8%
EO Items & Discontinued Operations	0.0%	0.0%	0.0%
Net Income	3.4%	3.4%	3.8%

Statement of Cash Flow

- **Cash Flows From Operating Activities**
  - Net Cash Generated From Selling Product or Service
- **Cash Flows From Investing Activities**
  - Net Cash From Investments In or Disposition of Fixed Assets or Acquisitions
- **Cash Flows From Financing Activities**
  - Cash From Sources of Funding

(in millions of USD)	12 Months ending January 31,		
	2001	2002	2003
Net Income	1,264	1,368	1,654
Depreciation and Amortization	940	1,079	1,212
Other non-cash adjustments	34	59	790
Change in non-cash working capital	-333	-514	-2,066
Cash Flow from Operations	1,905	1,992	1,590
Investing Activities			
Disposal of Fixed Assets	57	32	32
Capital Expenditures for PPE	-2,528	-3,163	-3,221
Other Investing Activities	-4	-179	0
Cash Flow from Investing	-2,475	-3,310	-3,189
Financing Activities			
Dividends	-190	-203	-216
Short-Term Debt	245	-8	0
Long-Term Debt	1,194	1,648	2,062
Capital Stock	-585	-20	-14
Other Financing Activities	42	44	6
Cash Flow from Investing	706	1,461	1,858
Beginning Cash Balance	220	356	499
Net Change in Cash	136	143	259
Ending Cash Balance	356	499	758

Financial Statement Links

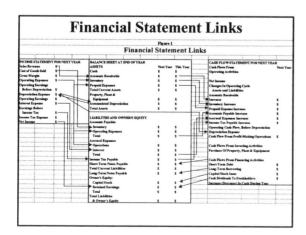

Figure 1
Financial Statement Links

Financial Statement Analysis

Financial Statement Analysis

This module shows how to use financial ratios by firms to measure and monitor firm performance. Objectives include:

(1) A <u>framework for performing a financial statement analysis</u> to gauge the health and performance of a business;
(2) An understanding of not only how to compute <u>financial ratios</u>, but also what they mean;
(3) How to employ the <u>Strategic Profit Model</u> as an overall assessment of profit, asset, and financial management.
(4) Analyze the financial statements of Target Corp. to <u>assess its performance, growth, and value relative to WalMart</u>.

Basic Financial Analysis

- **Liquidity Ratios**

- **Activity Measures**

- **Leverage Ratios**

- **Profitability Measures**

- **Valuation Ratios**

Financial Statements

Liquidity Ratios

- Measures Firm's Ability to Meet Short-Term Obligations
- Closely Related to Size and Composition of Working Capital Position
- Other Things Equal, Higher Working Capital Implies More Liquid Position

Current Ratio

- Indicates Amount of Current Assets Available to <u>Meet Maturing Obligations</u> Listed Under Current Liabilities
- Creditors Look At Ratio to Judge <u>"Cushion"</u> Between Current Obligations and Firm's Liquid Assets

$$\frac{\text{CURRENT ASSETS}}{\text{CURRENT LIABILITIES}}$$

Quick Ratio

- Also Known As Acid-Test Ratio
- More Conservative Measure of Liquidity
- Takes Inventory Off Before Measuring Liquidity
- Inventory Cannot Be Used to Readily Settle Claims

Financial Statements
Liquidity Ratios

Liquidity Ratios	Target	WalMart
Current Ratio = Current Assets/Current Liabilities		0.93
Quick Ratio = (Curr. Assets - Inventory)/Curr. Liabilities		0.17

Activity Ratios

- Asset Utilization Ratios
- Measures How Well Firm Uses Productive Resources
- Related to Amount of Sales Generated Per Dollar Invested In Particular Asset
- Related to Receivables, Inventory, Total Assets

Inventory Turnover

- Index of How Fast Goods Flow Through Inventory
- For Retail Companies: From Purchase to Sale
- For Manufacturing Company: From Raw Material to Sale
- Computed By Dividing Cost of Goods Sold (COGS) By Inventory

Receivables Turnover

- Measures Number of Times Receivables Turn Over During the Year
- Higher It Is, Shorter the Time Between Sales and Collection
- Indicates How Well Firm Manages Credit and Collection Policies

Payables Turnover

- Measures Number of Times Payables Turn Over During the Year
- Lower It Is, Longer the Time Company Takes to Pay Its Creditors
- Indicates How Well Firm Manages Its Payables

Financial Statements
Activity Ratios

Activity Ratios	Target	WalMart
Total Asset Turnover (TAT) = Sales/Total Assets	#	2.60x
Inventory Turnover = CGS/Inventory		7.71x
Days Sales in Inventory (DSI) = 365/Inventory Turnover		47.36
Receivables Turnover = Sales/Receivables		116.95x
Days Sales Outstanding (DSO) 365/Receivables Turnover Also known as the Average Collection Period		3.12
Payables Turnover = CGS/Payables		11.19x
Days Payables Outstanding (DPO) = 365/Payables Turnover		32.61
Cash Conversion Cycle = DSI + DSO (ACP) - DPO		17.87

Financial Leverage Ratios

■ Measure Risk Focusing On Financing Mix

■ Examine Extent to Which Firm Uses Debt to Finance Operations

■ Examine Balance Sheet: Higher Leverage Result In Higher Risk

■ Examine Income Statement: Coverage Ratios

Times Interest Earned

■ Measures Firm's Ability to Handle Debt

■ More Important Than Level of Debt Itself

■ Ratio Indicates Number of Times Firm's Operating Earnings (EBIT) Can "Cover" Its Interest Expense

Financial Statements
Financial Leverage Ratios

Leverage Ratios	Target	WalMart
Total Debt Ratio = Total Assets - Total Book Equity/Total Assets		0.58
Debt/Equity Ratio = Long-Term Debt/Book Value of Equity		0.42
Equity Multiplier (LM) = Total Assets/Book Value of Equity		2.41
Times Interest Earned = Earnings Before Interest and Taxes/Interest		14.75x

Profitability Ratios

- ■ Also Known As Operating Ratios
- ■ Vital In Assessing Managers' Performance
- ■ Examples:
- ■ Profit Margin
- ■ Return on Assets
- ■ Return on Equity

Profit Margin

- ■ Measures Firm's Ability to Control Its Expenses In Relation to Sales
- ■ Declining Margin Normally an Indication of Increasing Expense and/or Decreasing Sales
- ■ Useful to Investors For Measuring Manager's Performance

ROA and ROE

- ROA – Return on Assets
- Focuses on Earning Power of Going Operations and Assets
- ROE – Return on Equity
- Measures Return on Stockholders' Equity
- Increase In ROA and ROE Often Result In Stock Price Appreciation

---

Financial Statements
Profitability Ratios

Profitability Ratios	Target	WalMart
Profit Margin (Return on Sales ROS) = Net Profits After Tax/Sales		3.26%
Gross Profit Margin = Gross Profit/Sales		22.18%
Operating Profit Margin = Operating Profit/Sales		5.53%
Return on Assets (ROA) = Net Profits After Tax/Total Assets		8.49%
Return on Equity (ROE) = Net Profits After Tax/Book Value of Equity		20.44%

Valuation Ratios

- Determine Value Investors Place On Company
- Examples:
- Price/Earnings Ratio (P/E)
- Market-to-Book Ratio
- Market Capitalization

Financial Statements
Market Valuation Ratios

Market Value Ratios	Target	WalMart
Price/Earnings Ratio =		31.82
Stock Price/Earnings Per Share		
Stock Price = 38.00	EPS - 1.82	
Market-to-Book Ratio =		6.49x
Stock Price/Book Value Per Share		
	BVPS = 10.40	
Dividend Yield =		0.52%
Dividend Per Share/Stock Price		
	DPS = 0.24	
Market Capitalization =		$237,005,000,000
Stock Price * # of Shares Outstanding	# of shares = 908M	

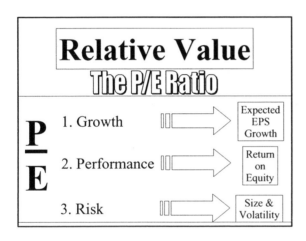

Relative Value
The P/E Ratio

$\dfrac{P}{E}$

1. Growth ▷ Expected EPS Growth

2. Performance ▷ Return on Equity

3. Risk ▷ Size & Volatility

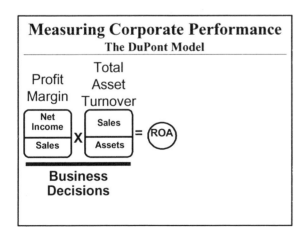

Measuring Corporate Performance
The DuPont Model

Profit Margin

Total Asset Turnover

$$\frac{\text{Net Income}}{\text{Sales}} \times \frac{\text{Sales}}{\text{Assets}} = \text{ROA}$$

Business Decisions

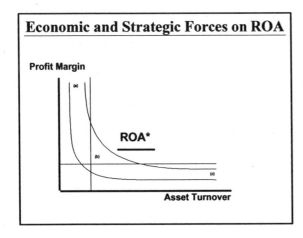

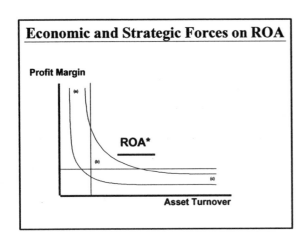

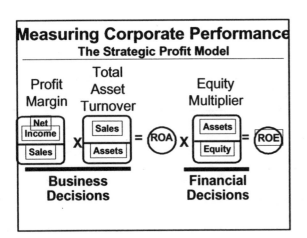

Measuring Corporate Performance
The Strategic Profit Model
ROS * Turnover = ROA * Leverage = ROE

Financial Ethics

Reading the Headlines

THE WALL STREET JOURNAL

Dirty Rotten Numbers

Is It the Shareholder Slaughter

Anatomy of a Shareholder Bottom Line or Better

Accounting Casts Its Shadow

Accounting Alchemy When Earnings Aren't

You Can't Believe the Numbers

Accounting Acrobatics

Financial Shenanigans

Slide 1

Slide 2

Financial Ethics: GAAP vs. GAP

GAAP

Generally Accepted Accounting Principles
Issued by FASB; Ultimate Regulation is by the SEC

GAP

Slide 3

The Financial Numbers Game

- **Aggressive accounting** - A forceful and intentional choice and **application of accounting principles done in an effort to achieve desired results**, typically higher current earnings, whether the practices followed are in accordance with GAAP or not

- **Earnings management** - The active manipulation of **earnings toward a predetermined target**, which may be set by management, a forecast made by analysts, or an amount that is consistent with a smoother, more sustainable earnings stream

- **Income smoothing** - A form of earnings management designed **to remove peaks and valleys** from a normal earnings series, including steps to reduce and "store" profits during good years for use during slower years

- **Fraudulent financial reporting** - Intentional **misstatements or omissions** of amounts or disclosures in financial statements, done to deceive financial statement users, that are determined to be fraudulent by an administrative, civil, or criminal proceeding

- **Creative accounting practices** - **Any and all steps used to play the financial numbers game**, including the aggressive choice and application of accounting principles fraudulent financial reporting, and any steps taken toward earnings management or income smoothing

Source: Charles Mulford and Eugene Comiskey, *The Financial Numbers Game* (John Wiley & Sons, 2002).

Cooking the Books

Schilit's Seven Financial Shenanigans

1. **Recording revenue too soon**
2. **Recording bogus revenue**
3. **Boosting income with one-time gains**
4. **Shifting current expenses to a later or earlier period**
5. **Failing to disclose all liabilities**
6. **Shifting current income to a later period**
7. **Shifting future expenses into the current period**

Source: Howard Schilit, *Financial Shenanigans* (McGraw Hill, 2002).

No. 1 - Recording Revenue Too Soon

Revenue Should be Recognized Once an Exchange has Occurred

No. 1 - Recording Revenue Too Soon

Shipping goods before sale is finalized

1. Billing in advance
2. Shipping defective goods
3. Using an aggressive revenue approach

No. 1 - Recording Revenue Too Soon

Recording revenue when important uncertainties exist

1. Is the sale with or without recourse?

2. Does the buyer have financing to pay?

3. Is there an obligation by the buyer to pay?

Recording revenue before shipment or customer's unconditional acceptance

Recording revenue although customer is not obligated to pay

Selling to an affiliated party

Giving customer something of value as a quid pro quo

No. 1 - Recording Revenue Too Soon

Recording revenue when future services are still due

1. Booking future revenue

Enron

Booked PV of differences between 5 year sales contract to utility & 5 year purchase contract from supplier at time of inception.

No. 2 - Recording Bogus Revenue

Revenue Should be Recognized Once an Exchange has Occurred

No. 2 - Recording Bogus Revenue

Management records refunds from suppliers as revenue

Recording sales lacking economic substance – side agreements

Recording cash received from lender as revenue

Recording investment income as revenue

Recording as revenue supplier rebates tied to future required purchases

Release revenue improperly "held back" before a merger

Inventory games

Reliant Resources

Recorded Bogus Revenue

Revenue for the years 1999-2001 was overstated by $7.8 billion due to the recording of "round-trip" energy trades. These types of energy trades involved Reliant Energy buying and then selling an equal amount of a commodity in order to artificially inflate revenues.

No. 3 - Boosting Income with One-Time Gains

Revenue Should be Recognized Once an Exchange has Occurred and Similarly, Report Gains only after an Exchange has taken Place

No. 3 - Boosting Income with One-Time Gains

We bring good things to life.

Management sells undervalued asset

Recording gains selling assets recorded at deflated book value

Including investment income or gains as revenue

Including investment income as reduction in operating expenses

Creating income by reclassification of investment gains s

No. 4 – Shift Expenses to a Later Period

Capitalize Costs that Produce a Future Benefit and Expense Those that Produce no Such Benefit

---

No. 4 – Shift Expenses to a Later Period

Management improperly capitalizes costs

1. Start-up costs
2. R&D costs
3. Advertising expenditures
4. Administrative costs

No. 4 – Shift Expenses to a Later Period	
	Management depreciates or amortizes costs too slowly
	1. Excessively long amortization periods
	2. Increases in depreciation /amortization schedules
	Key Issues:
	What is normal industry practice?
	Is the industry experiencing rapid technological change?

_____

_____

_____

_____

_____

_____

_____

No. 4 – Shift Expenses to a Later Period	
	Management fails to write-off worthless assets
	Changing accounting policies and shift current expenses to an earlier period
	Amortizing costs too slowly
	Releasing asset reserves into income

_____

_____

_____

_____

_____

_____

Waste Management
A Case Study in Value Destruction

Accounting Issues
Avoiding depreciation expenses on garbage trucks
Assigning arbitrary salvage values to assets that previously had no salvage value
Failing to record expenses of landfills as they were filled with waste
Refusing to record expenses of unsuccessful and abandoned landfill projects
Established inflated environmental reserves
Improperly capitalized expenses
Failed to establish sufficient reserves to pay for income taxes and other expenses

Source: U.S. Securities and Exchange Commission, 26 March 2002: 2002: 44

WORLDCOM

CREATIVE ACCOUNTING

By booking certain costs as a capital expense, WorldCom was able to boost its bottom line. A look at how the company conducted such accounting in 2001.

WorldCom's accounting

1. Accounts $3.1 billion in 'line costs,' including telecom access and transport charges, as capital expenditure.
2. Plans to amortize $3.1 billion over a period of time, possibly as much as 10 years.
3. Reports net income of $1.38 billion for 2001.

Expense:
- Capital Expense
- Operating Expense
- Amortization
- Cost of Business
- Higher Net Income
- Lower Net Income

Generally accepted accounting principles

1. The $3.1 billion 'line-cost' expense is booked as an operating expense.
2. The entire $3.1 billion would have been counted as a cost of business for that quarter.
3. Net income for 2001 would have been a loss, amount to be determined.

No. 5 – Fail to Record / Disclose all Liabilities

A Firm incurs a Liability if it has an Obligation to make Future Sacrifices

No. 5 – Fail to Record / Disclose all Liabilities

Failing to record expenses (and related liabilities) when future obligations remain

Reducing liabilities by changing accounting assumptions

Releasing questionable liability reserves into income

Creating sham rebates

Recording revenue when cash is received, yet future obligations remain

No. 5 – Fail to Record / Disclose all Liabilities

Management fails to accrue expected or contingent liabilities

Accrue loss when:
» There is a probable loss
» The amount is reasonably estimated

No. 5 – Fail to Record / Disclose all Liabilities

Management engages in transactions to keep debt off the books

FASB attempting to correct:
» Swaps
» In-substance defeasance of debt
» Defined-benefit pensions
» Operating leases
» Subs & joint ventures
» Special purpose entities

No. 6 – Shift Current Income to a Later Period

Record Revenue/Expenses in the Period in Which it is Earned

No. 6 – Shift Current Income to a Later Period

Management creates reserves to shift income to a later period

Cookie-Jar Reserves
Smooth income through the use of reserves

Improperly holding back revenue just before an acquisition closes

No. 7 – Shift Future Expenses to the Current Period

> **Charge Expenses Against
> Income in the Period in Which
> the Benefit is Received**

No. 7 – Shift Future Expenses to the Current Period

**Management accelerates
discretionary expenses into
the current period**

Prepayment of operating
expenses

Shorter "life" means higher
expense each period

Improperly write off in-
process R&D costs from
acquisition

No. 7 – Shift Future Expenses to the Current Period

**Management has the firm
"take the big bath"**

New management often
writes-off old projects to
relieve future periods of
the expenses

Large nonrecurring gains
offset with large expenses,
or vice versa

The Financial Life Cycle of the Firm: From Raising Capital to Acquisitions, Mergers and Spinoffs

The Financial
Life Cycle

The Financial Life Cycle

This module examines the financial life cycle of a firm.
It covers the capital raising process, the primary securities
market, and mergers and acquisitions. Objectives for
this module include:

(1) Understanding the role of the SEC as the regulator
    of the primary securities markets;
(2) Review the financing life cycle and sources of
    capital of a firm;
(3) Explore the primary securities market and the
    securities issuance process;
(4) Identify current themes and trends in the primary
    securities market
(5) Provide an introduction to mergers and acquisitions.

Financial Facts of the Day

The Most Valuable Companies in the World
Market Value of Common Stock

The SEC as Regulator

Primary Roles/Goals

1. Protect Investors

2. Information Disclosure

3. Operational and Pricing Efficiency of Security Markets

4. Fair and Orderly Markets

The SEC as Regulator

Procedural Elements of the SEC

1. Rules and Regulations

2. Enforcement Action

3. Provide for Full and Fair Disclosure of Information
   - Quarterly and Annual Filing Requirements

Nvidia Corporation Is The Worldwide Leader Of Graphics Processors and Media Communications Devices

Designs, Develops and Markets 3D Graphics Processors, Graphics Processing Units, And Related Software For Every Type Of Desktop Personal Computer

Increases in Revenue and Net Income Reflect Strong Demand For New Products At Higher Average Selling Prices

Financial Data

Market Cap $6.981 billion

Revenue: 1999- $158M, 2000- $374.5M, 2001- $735M

<u>Contract Info</u>

Contract Involving Manufacture Of Graphics Chip For Microsoft's Xbox

Share Price More Than Doubled After Contract Announcement On March 10, 2000

Production of Chips Began In May, Could Bring in Revenue Of $2 billion

<u>Case Info</u>

Charges Brought Against 15 People In November 2001

Case Involves All Lower-Level Employees And Their Friends/Relatives

Insiders Alleged To Have Earned $1.7

2 Defendants Have Settled Charges By Returning Gains, Without Admitting Wrongdoing

---

Time Line of Significant Events

March 6, 2000
Employees Receive
Follow-Up Message
Reminding Them Of
Confidentiality

March 00'   August 00'   November 00'

The SEC as Regulator

William Donaldson, SEC Chairman

Grading The **Chairman**

B+ **ENFORCEMENT** Donaldson's hang-'em-high stance has given enforcers more manpower and free rein to pursue securities fraudsters. The result: steep fines, bans on errant execs from serving as officers and directors, and a string of Enron settlements.

A **AGENCY MORALE** The SEC isn't the butt of jokes on late-night talk shows anymore, but New York Attorney General Eliot Spitzer still uses the agency as his whipping boy on occasion.

B- **STOCK MARKETS** Donaldson pressured the NYSE to 'fess up on executive pay and send former CEO Grasso packing. But knotty issues about how stocks are traded and markets interact have languished.

I **SHAREHOLDER DEMOCRACY** Facing down Corporate America, Donaldson vows to make it easier for shareholders to nominate directors if companies ignore investor concerns. Incomplete so far, but action is expected by late spring.

I **MUTUAL FUNDS** The SEC was slow to respond to abuses in the industry, but now it's preparing a slew of reforms to curb unsavory trading practices and make fees and costs more transparent.

Elliott Spitzer as Market Regulator

Wall Street Analysts
$1.5B Settlement With
Major Brokerage Firms
For Tainted Research

Mutual Funds
Settlements With Major
Investment Companies who
Allowed Favored Customers
To Execute 'Market Timing'
Trades

Elliot Spitzer
Attorney General
New York

The Financing Life Cycle

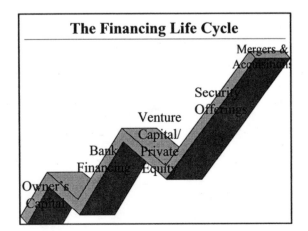

Owner's Capital

Bank Financing

Venture Capital/ Private Equity

Security Offerings

Mergers & Acquisitions

The Financing Life Cycle

Owners Capital
Initial Capital Investment
of Owners

Bank Financing
Loans and Lines-of-Credit
From Financial Institutions

Venture Capital
Equity Investments
by Investors in
Private Companies

Venture Capital Financing

Risk Capital
Debt/Equity Capital Required
for Growth Once Bank
Financing is Unavailable

Required Returns
20 - 50 Percent Expected
Return Depending on Stage
VC Exit Strategy (Sell/IPO)

Types of Financing
Depends on Financing Stage

How Venture Capital Works

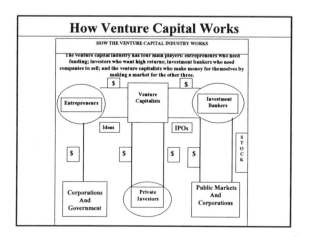

Venture Capital Financing

Seed/Startup Funding
Earliest stage of business, typically no operating history. Investment is based on a business plan, the management group backgrounds along with the market and financial projections.

First Round Funding
Typically funding that accomodates growth. Company may have finished R&D. Funding is often in the form of convertible bond.

Intermediate/Second Round Funding
Maturing company where a future leveraged buyout, merger or acquisition and/or initial public offering is a viable option.

Later Stage Funding
Mature company where funds are needed to support major expansion or new product development. Company is profitable or breakeven.

Venture Capital Financing

Later Stage Funding
Mature company where funds are needed to support major expansion or new product development. Company is profitable or breakeven.

Equity Loan
Offer of an ownership position to induce the loan or can be a note that has an option to convert from debt to equity.

Mezzanine Funding
Company's progress makes positioning for an Initial Public Offering viable. Venture funds are used to support the IPO.

The Lifecycle of a Venture Capital Deal

CacheFlow

◆ **March 13, 1996** - CacheFlow Founded by Michael Malcolm with $1M from 'Angels'. Design and Produce a a Caching Appliance for Faster Internet Pages

◆ **October 1996** - Benchmark Capital Buys 25% of CacheFlow (3.2M 'A' Shares @ $.875). Remaining 75% Owned by Management and Angels

◆ **Jan-Nov 1997** - Development and Testing of Product - Ready

◆ **December 1997** - Still with no Revenues, US Venture Partners Pays $6 M ('B' Shares @ $2.28) for 17% of Firm. Benchmark Chips in $1.8M to Retain 25%

◆ **May 1998** - Revenues of $800,000 for Year

The Lifecycle of a Venture Capital Deal

CacheFlow

◆ **June 1998**　　　- Investment Bankers Come Calling

◆ **March 1999**　　- Tech Exec Brian NeSmith Hired as CEO.
　　　　　　　　　　New VC Financing - 'C' Shares @ $4.575/Share
　　　　　　　　　　Technology X-Over Ventures - $8.7M for 7%
　　　　　　　　　　Benchmark - $3.4M to Retain 18%
　　　　　　　　　　US Venture Partners - $2.1M to Retain 12%

◆ **August 1999**　　- MSDW and CSFB Hired as Investment Bankers

◆ **September 1999** - S-1 Filed - 5M Shares or 15.6% of Company
　　　　　　　　　　Revenues - $3.8 M - Net Loss - (13.2M)

◆ **November 1999**　- IPO @ $24 on Nov 19

The Lifecycle of a Venture Capital Deal

CacheFlow

◆ **November 19, 1999**　- CacheFlow Stock Closes @ $126/Share on First Day of Trading

　　　　　　　　　　Stock Performance
　　　　　　　　　　'A' Shares - $.875 - $126 - 14,342%
　　　　　　　　　　'B' Shares - $2.28 - $126 - 5,491%
　　　　　　　　　　'C' Shares - $4.575 - $126 - 2,662%

◆ **April 2000**　　- Stock @ $112 - VC Investment Performance
　　　　　　　　　　Benchmark - $8.0M to $537M
　　　　　　　　　　US Venture Partners - $8.1M to $351M
　　　　　　　　　　Technology X-Over Ventures - $8.7M to $213M
　　　　　　　　　　Mr. Malcolm - 5.1M Shares - $576M

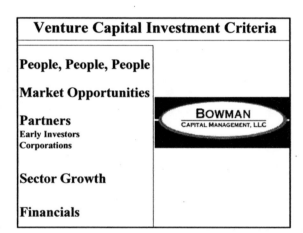

Venture Capital Investment Criteria

People, People, People

Market Opportunities

Partners
Early Investors
Corporations

Sector Growth

Financials

BOWMAN
CAPITAL MANAGEMENT, LLC

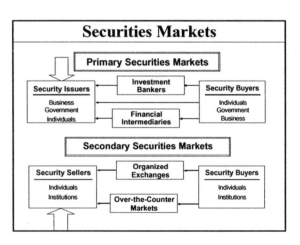

Securities Markets

Primary Securities Markets

Security Issuers
Business
Government
Individuals

Investment Bankers

Security Buyers
Individuals
Government
Business

Financial Intermediaries

Secondary Securities Markets

Security Sellers
Individuals
Institutions

Organized Exchanges

Security Buyers
Individuals
Institutions

Over-the-Counter Markets

The Role of Securities Markets

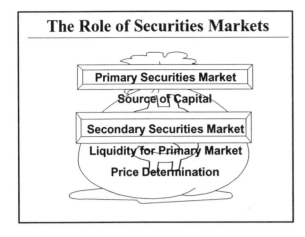

Primary Securities Market
Source of Capital

Secondary Securities Market
Liquidity for Primary Market
Price Determination

The Financing Life Cycle

Initial Public Offering (IPO)
Initial Public Sale of Common Stock to Investors

Seasoned Offerings
Subsequent Sales of Common Stock to Investors

Also Known as Secondary Offerings

ANATOMY OF A DEAL

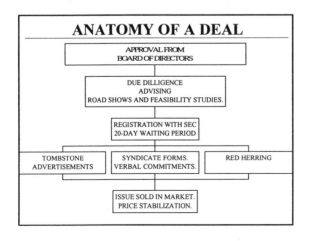

APPROVAL FROM
BOARD OF DIRECTORS

DUE DILLIGENCE
ADVISING
ROAD SHOWS AND FEASIBILITY STUDIES.

REGISTRATION WITH SEC
20-DAY WAITING PERIOD

TOMBSTONE
ADVERTISEMENTS

SYNDICATE FORMS.
VERBAL COMMITMENTS.

RED HERRING

ISSUE SOLD IN MARKET.
PRICE STABILIZATION.

The Primary Securities Markets

Investment Banking and Security Issuances

1. Advising

2. Origination (Securities Act of 1933)
   – Due Diligence, Registration Statement, Prospectus

3. Syndicate Formation, Underwriting, and Price Stabilization

---

Underwriting Syndicate

Issuing Firm

Investment Bank

Managing Investment Bank

Investment Bank

Selling Group of Brokers and Dealers

Investors

The Primary Securities Market
Security Issuances

◆ **IPOs Versus Secondary Offerings**
- IPO - Initial Sale of Common Stock to Investors in Market
- Secondary Offering - Sales of Common Stock by Publicly-Held Firms

◆ **Registration Statement**
- Filed with the SEC Prior to Selling Securities to Investors

◆ **Prospectus**
Selling Document for Securities

The Primary Securities Market
Security Issuances

- ◆ **Red Herring**
  Preliminary Prospectus

- ◆ **"Tombstones"**
  Issue Advertisement

- ◆ **Green Shoe**
  Underwriter Option to Sell
  15% More Shares

- ◆ **Negotiated Offerings**
  - **Underwritings**
  - **Best Efforts and**
    Stand-by Offerings

Public Offering of Securities

Negotiated Sale
- **Underwritings**
- **Best Efforts**
- **Standby**

Competitive Bid

The Primary Securities Market
The Costs of Security Issuances

→ **Underwriting Spread**
The Difference Between the
Price the Issuer Receives
and the Offer Price

→ **Other Direct Expenses**
Printing and Legal Expenses

→ **Indirect Expenses**
Company Costs Associated
with a Security Issue

Initial Public Offerings

Why Go Public? (IPO)
Capital to Execute Business Plan
Liquidity for Owners
Stock for Compensation and
  Acquisitions
Marketing and Branding
  Opportunity
Capital Market Access

_____

_____

_____

_____

_____

_____

_____

On February 10, 2000
Webmethods went Public by
Selling 4.7M Shares to Investors
at $35 per Share ($165M)

Company Received $32.76 After
$2.24 Underwriting Spread

End-of-First Day Price: $212 (+508%)

Company Develops XML
Software Applications that
Allows Electronic Communications
Between Large Divergent
Computer Systems

Facilitates B-2-B Commerce

1999 Sales - $15M
1999 Loss - ($10M)

_____

_____

_____

_____

_____

_____

_____

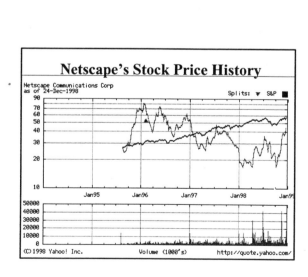

Netscape's Stock Price History

Netscape Communications Corp
as of 24-Dec-1998

Splits: ▼ S&P ■

90
70
60
50
40
30
20

10

Jan95   Jan96   Jan97   Jan98   Jan99

50000
40000
30000
20000
10000
0

(C) 1998 Yahoo! Inc.   Volume (1000's)   http://quote.yahoo.com/

The IPO Hall of Fame

VA Linux Systems	+733%
Theglobe.com	+606%
Foundry Networks	+525%
Webmethods	+508%
FreeMarkets	+483%
Cobalt Networks	+482%
Akamai Tech	+458%
CacheFlow	+427%
Sycamore Networks	+386%
Ask Jeevesom	+364%
Finisar	+357%
Crossroads Systems	+337%
Priceline.com	+331%
Wireless Facilities	+313%
Calico Commerce	+300%

Long Shots

	VA LINUX	
1999 Sales	$47.1	$18.6
1999 EPS	-1.68	-2.06
1999 ROE	-63.5%	-50.8%
Expected EPS Growth	NMF	NMF
Stock Price	$65	$6
Market Capitalization	$2.7B	$171M
Price/Earnings Ratio	NMF	NMF

**Start-Up Businesses that have Attracted Much Investor Interest
Despite Not Demonstrating a Viable and Profitable Business Model**

The Appeal of IPOs

- ◆ IPOs Appeal to Investors Due to Their Potential for High Returns

- ◆ Examples:

Company	Annual Return	$1,000 Worth Today
Microsoft (1986)	46%	$113,350
Dell (1988)	77%	$350,000
AOL (1992)	115%	$100,000
Lucent (1996)	100%	$5,660

The Primary Securities Market
Initial Public Offerings (IPOs)

→ The Initial Sale of Common Stock to the Public by a Company

→ The Average First Day Return (15%) is Evidence of Underpricing

→ The Winner's Curse - The Average Investor Does Not Get the First Day Return

→ The Long-Term (3-Year) Adjusted Performance of IPOs is Negative

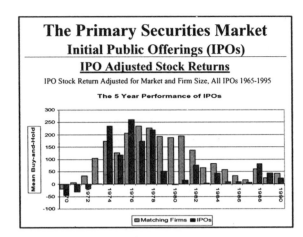

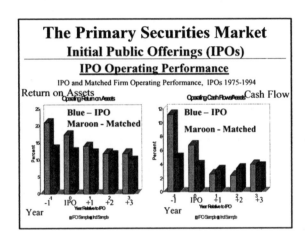

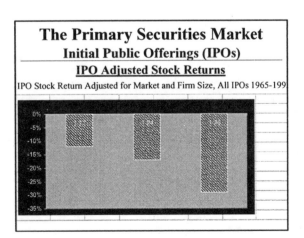

The Primary Securities Market
Seasoned/Secondary Offerings

➔ **The Sale of New Common Stock by a Public Company**

➔ **Using Equity Markets as a Source of Capital to Meet Financing Needs**

➔ **The Average Return at the Announcement is -3.0%**

➔ **Seasoned Issues Are a Negative Signal to Investors**

Lycos, the Internet Portal Company, went Public at $8 on 4/16/96. On January 4, 2000, the Company Filed a Registration Statement with the SEC to Sell 5 Million Shares of Common Stock. The Stated Use of the Funds are for General Corporate Purposes and Acquisitions. At the time, the Stock was Selling at $81.

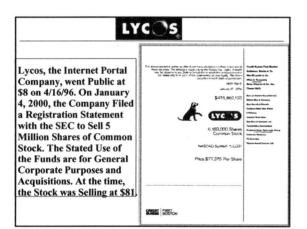

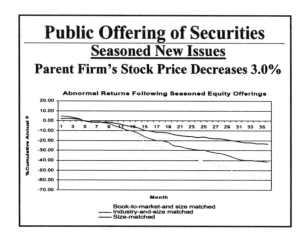

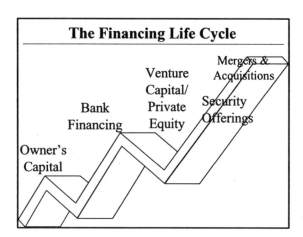

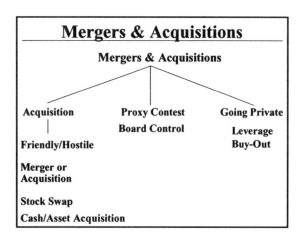

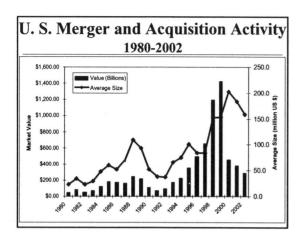

U. S. Merger and Acquisition Activity
1980-2002

Corporate Takeovers:
The 1980s Versus the 1990s

1980s	1990s
→ Financial Deals	→ Strategic, Convergence, Global
→ Deals were Hostile	→ Deals are Friendly
→ Debt Financed	→ Stock Financed
→ Availability of Financing Led to 1990s Merger Wave	→ Industry Restructuring has Added to 1990s Merger Wave
→ Bad Press	→ Good Press

Business Week

THE MERGER

HANGOVER

How most big acquisitions have destroyed Shareholder value

BIG DEALS

Megamergers have done little for buyers' share prices. A year later, many lagged their peers or just kept pace

BUYER	INDUSTRY	TARGET	DATE	VALUE (BILLIONS)	PREMIUM**	SELLER INITIAL	BUYER INITIAL	BUYER 1 YEAR
AMERICA ONLINE	INTERNET SOFTWARE	TIME WARNER	1/00	$165.9	55.8%	11%	1%	17%
PFIZER	PHARMACEUTICALS	WARNER-LAMBERT	11/99	93.9	29.7	20	-12	1
EXXON	OIL & GAS	MOBIL	12/98	77.2	34.2	18	1	-5
TRAVELERS GROUP (1)	INSURANCE	CITICORP	4/98	70.0	10.4	8	6	2
SBC COMMUNICATIONS	TELECOM SVCS.	AMERITECH	5/98	61.2	23.3	3	-8	-19
NATIONSBANK (2)	BANKS	BANKAMERICA	4/98	59.3	48.4	2	4	4
AT&T	TELECOM SVCS.	MEDIAONE GROUP	4/99	55.8	24.3	18	-6	-4
BELL ATLANTIC (3)	TELECOM SVCS.	GTE	7/98	52.8	3.8	-1	5	6
VIACOM	MEDIA	CBS	9/99	40.4	4.0	5	6	32
QWEST COMMUNICATIONS	TELECOM SVCS.	US WEST	6/99	40.3	27.5	4	-23	21
DAIMLER-BENZ	AUTOMOBILES	CHRYSLER	5/98	38.6	54.3	16	-6	-30
JDS UNIPHASE	COMMUNICATIONS EQUIP	SDL	7/00	38.1	50.7	24	-19	-44
CHASE MANHATTAN (4)	FINANCIAL	J.P. MORGAN	9/00	36.3	28.9	1	-18	-18
CHEVRON	OIL & GAS	TEXACO	10/00	35.8	24.8	12	-3	10
NORWEST (5)	BANKS	WELLS FARGO	6/98	33.9	0.9	-8	-11	10

*Price of offer when announced. **Difference between the offer price and the seller's market price one week before the announcement. ***Percentage-point difference between company returns and return of S&P 500 peers from one week before announcement to one week (initial) and one year after. Current names: (1) Citigroup (2) Bank of America (3) Verizon (4) J.P. Morgan Chase (5) Wells Fargo
Data: Standard & Poor's, Mergerstat, Boston Consulting Group Inc., Thomson Financial

The Value Creation Challenge of Acquisitions

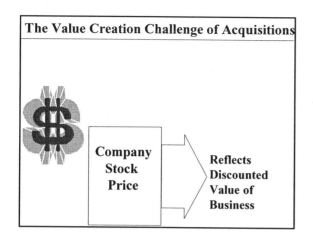

Company Stock Price → Reflects Discounted Value of Business

Sources of Synergy Value

- Cost Savings
  - E.g. Economies of Scale
- Revenue Enhancements
  - E.g. Complementary Products
- Process Improvements
  - E.g. Transfer of Best Practices
- Financial Engineering
  - E.g. Reduced Cost of Capital

Stock Market Reaction to Acquisitions

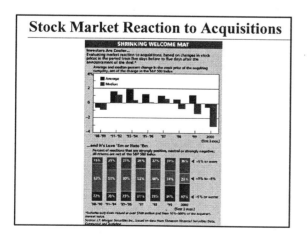

Why Do Mergers Fail?

- Overpay by Offering a Large Premium, Which Hands the Bulk of Future Gains from the Merger to Shareholders of the Target Company

- Overestimate Cost Savings From Operating Synergies and Revenue Gains from Marketing Synergies

- Slow to Integrate Operations After Merger, Frustrating Customers and Employees

- Obsessed with Cost-Cutting and Not Dealing with Resolving Culture Conflicts

Equity Carve-Outs and Spinoffs

Reverse Merger
Break a Company Up by:
1. Equity Carve Out – IPO In a Subsidiary
2. Spin-Off a Subsidiary By Distributing Shares in The Form of a Dividend

AT&T - Lucent-NCR

AT&T
$50B Telecom Service Company

AT&T Sold 17% of Lucent in a $3.1B IPO on April 3, 1996

AT&T Spun-Off NCR by Distributing NCR Shares to its Shareholders on December 31, 1996

Lucent Technologies
$20B Telecom Equipment Company
AT&T Distributed the Remaining 83% to its Shareholders on Sept. 29, 1996 in a Tax-Free Spinoff

NCR
$6B Maker of Information Technology Products

Equity Carve Outs

◆ An Initial Public Offering (IPO) for Some Portion of a Wholly-Owned Subsidiary

◆ Generally the Parent Retains at Least 80% Ownership to Qualify for Tax Consolidation and Future Tax-Free Spinoff

◆ Either the Parent or the Subsidiary Can Offer the Shares

◆ Requires S-1 Registration

Equity Carve Outs

AT&T - Lucent Technologies

Hewlett Packard – Agilent Technologies

3 Com - Palm

DuPont - Conoco

Sears - Allstate Insurance

The Limited - Intimate Brands

Thermal Electron - 22 ECOs

Spinoffs

◆ A Stock Dividend in the Form of the Stock of a Subsidiary

◆ Usually Structured to Meet IRC Section 355 Requirements as a Tax-Free Spinoff
  - Active Business
  - Business Purpose
  - At Lease 80% Spunoff

◆ Parent Stock Rises 2% at the Announcement On Average

◆ Requires Form 10 SEC Filing

Notable Spinoffs

Sprint - 360 Communications

ITT – ITT Industries – ITT Hartford

GM - EDS

Quaker Oats – Fisher-Price Toys

Pepsico - Tricon

General Mills - Darden Restaurants

Coors – ACX Technologies

Baxter International – Caremark

Pacific Telesis – Air Touch

Host Marriott – Marriott Intl.

American Express - Lehman Bros

Value Creation Through Spinoffs

Company Characteristics	Quaker Oats	Fisher-Price
Culture	Tight Controls	Entreprenueral
Capital Intensity	Low	High
Risk	Low	High

The Capital Markets

Capital Markets

Capital Markets

This module explores the role and the elements of the secondary securities market. Objectives for this module include:

(1) Understanding the <u>basic structure</u> of the secondary securities markets;
(2) Exploring the differences between the <u>organized exchanges and the over-the-counter</u> (OTC) market;
(3) Identifying <u>measures of the stock market</u> as well as current issues in the markets

Financial Fact of the Day

Performance of Recommended Stocks
Top-Tier Brokerage Firms – 1993-2002

And the Winner is ...

The Role of Financial Markets

- Mobilize Savings and Allocate Funds to Users On Basis of Expected Risk-Adjusted Returns

- Facilitate Risk Transfer

- Provide Liquidity

- Crucial Role In Valuing Financial Assets

_____

_____

_____

_____

_____

_____

Exchanges In Financial Markets

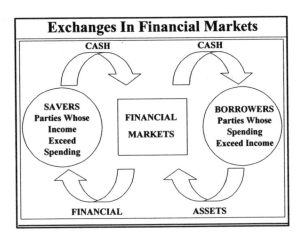

_____

_____

_____

_____

_____

_____

Well-Functioning Financial Markets

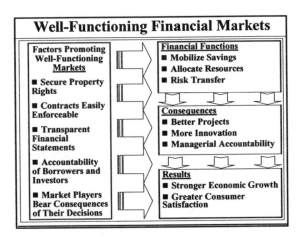

_____

_____

_____

_____

_____

Dealers vs. Brokers

- **Dealer Markets:** Individuals or Firms Facilitate Trades Between Buyers and Sellers

- **Brokered Markets:** Brokers Serve As Agents to Bring Buyers and Sellers Together

Capital Markets

- **Organized Exchange:** Actual Physical Place For Trading Securities
- **E.g., NYSE and American Stock Exchange**
- **Over-the-Counter Markets:** No Physical Location
- **Dealers Linked By Computer Network**
- **E.g., NASDAQ**

Capital Markets
Organized Exchanges

NYSE	The American Exchange
8 Regional Exchanges	
Listing Requirements	
Trading floor	
Specialist/ Open Auction System -	
Securities Traded	

Types of Orders

Market Order
An Order to Buy/Sell at the
Best Price When the Order
Reaches the Exchange

Buy 1000 WMT
at the Market

Limit Order
An Order to Buy/Sell at a
Specified Price

Buy 1000 WMT
at $57 (GTC)

The Secondary Securities Markets
Organized Exchanges

Specialist
A Trader Who Makes a Market
in One or More Securities and
is Charged with Maintaining
a Fair and Orderly Market
- Hold Inventory
- Buy/Sell Stock
- Maintain Limit Order Book

Trading Post
Position on Floor Where
Specialist Make Markets in
Securities

NYSE

Firm/Ownership	Total Common Stocks	Share by Dollar Value of Specialist Trades	No. of DJIA Stocks	Big Name Stocks
LaBranche & Co. (Publicly traded)	582	26.9%	9	3M; AT&T; Berkshire Hathaway; Delta Airlines
Spear, Leeds, & Kellogg Specialists (unit of Goldman Sachs	573	23.4%	3	Allianz AG; Fannie Mae; FedEx; IBM; MetLife
Fleet Specialists (unit of FleetBoston Financial)	435	20.3%	9	Coca-Cola; Home Depot; GE, GM; McDonald's; Sprint
Van Der Mioelen Specialists (publicly traded)	376	10.8%	3	Apache; Cendant; Disney; Harley-Davidson; IDT
Bear Wagner Specialists (minority partner: Bear Stearns	340	15.2%	4	Procter & Gamble; Citigroup; Deutsche Telekom; Merrill Lynch
Performance Specialist Group (privately held)	139	1.2%	0	CBC Entertainment; Illinois Tool Works; Sony (ADRs); Pep Boys
Susquehanna Specialists (privately held)	122	2.2%	0	Borders Group; IHOP; OfficeMax; Reebok

Organized Exchanges
The Specialist System

Exchange Floor

Orders → Open Auction ← Orders

Specialist

Trading Post

Orders ↗ ↖ Orders

◆ **Orders of Less Than 1,200 Shares -Designated Order Turnaround System (DOT)**
Orders Wired Directly to the Specialist's Computer and Executed at Market Price

◆ **Super DOT is an Improved Version of DOT**

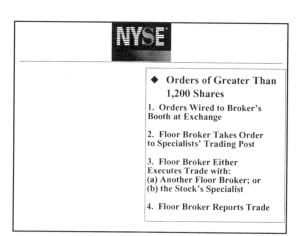

◆ **Orders of Greater Than 1,200 Shares**

1. Orders Wired to Broker's Booth at Exchange

2. Floor Broker Takes Order to Specialists' Trading Post

3. Floor Broker Either Executes Trade with:
(a) Another Floor Broker; or
(b) the Stock's Specialist

4. Floor Broker Reports Trade

Slide 1

Investor : Places an order to buy or sell shares of a company	Specialist Exposes the order in the Agency auction market
NYSE Member Brokerage Firm: Checks The customers account, quotes bid/ask Information and routes the order to the Trading floor	Floor Broker: Takes the order to the trading post where the stock is traded. Competes with other Brokers for the best price
Common Message Switch/Super DOT: CMS/SuperDot stores and routes the order to a broker's booth or directly to a specialist	Brokerage Firm: The Transaction is processed electronically crediting or debiting the customer's Account with the number of shares transacted
Trading Post: The order displays on the Specialist's screen, an order management system	Investor: Receives a trade confirmation From his firm
Broker's Booth: The firm's clerk receivbes the order The clerk notifies the firm's floor borker that an order has arrived	

Slide 2

NYSE

NYSE Facts	
No. of Listed Firms	2,744
Market Value	$14T
2003 Daily Volume	1,420M
2003 Seat Price	$1.9M
Security Firms	337
Average Stock Piece	$28
Average Trade Size	500
Listing Requirements Shareholders, Volume, Market Cap, Earnings	

Slide 3

Execution on the NYSE

Specialist
Lists Spread:

Bid
16 4/16
30,000

Ask
16 6/16
20,000

Capital Markets
The Over-The-Counter Market

The Over-the-Counter
Market (OTC)

Broker/Dealer System

The Competitive
Market Maker System

NASDAQ System

Securities Traded

Capital Markets
The Over-The-Counter Market

Security Dealer
Security Firms Who Makes a
Market in One or More Securities
Known as Marketmakers

NASDAQ
Automated Quotation System
Which Provides Dealer Bid and Ask
Quotes

Bid Prices
Price at Which Dealer will Buy

Ask Prices
Price at Which Dealer will Sell

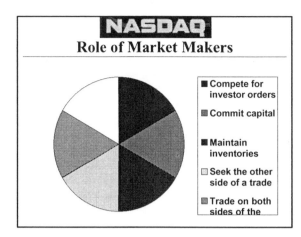

Role of Market Makers

- Compete for investor orders
- Commit capital
- Maintain inventories
- Seek the other side of a trade
- Trade on both sides of the

NASDAQ

The Anatomy of a Trade

1. Broker Obtains Bid/Ask Quotes on Stock from NASDAQ System

2. Broker Directs Order to Dealer Offering the Best Price
(a) Buy Order - Lowest Ask Price
(b) Sell Order - Highest Bid Price

3. Broker Confirms Trade

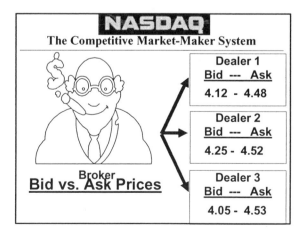

The Competitive Market-Maker System

Broker
Bid vs. Ask Prices

Dealer 1	
Bid ---	Ask
4.12 -	4.48

Dealer 2	
Bid ---	Ask
4.25 -	4.52

Dealer 3	
Bid ---	Ask
4.05 -	4.53

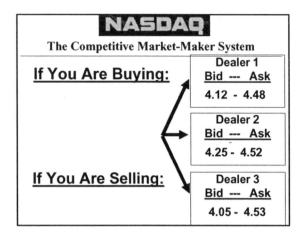

NASDAQ

The Competitive Market-Maker System

If You Are Buying:

If You Are Selling:

| Dealer 1 |
| Bid --- Ask |
| 4.12 - 4.48 |

| Dealer 2 |
| Bid --- Ask |
| 4.25 - 4.52 |

| Dealer 3 |
| Bid --- Ask |
| 4.05 - 4.53 |

Dealer Markets

Buyers & Sellers Evaluate Bids/Asks from Dealers

| Buyers of Stock Seek The Lowest Ask Price | Seller of Stock Seek The Highest Bid Price |

The Inside Spread is The Combination
Of the Lowest Ask and Highest Bid Prices

	Dealer 1	Dealer 2	Dealer 3	Dealer 4	Dealer 5	Dealer 6
Bid	20.90	20.94	20. 91	20.97	20.96	20.93
	800	300	500	200	400	300
Ask	21.15	21.18	21.20	21.17	21.19	21.18
	100	400	500	400	200	300
Spread	.25	.24	.29	.20	.23	.25

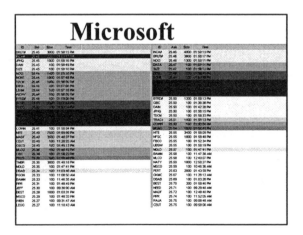

Microsoft

NASDAQ
Market Participants

Market Makers

individual dealers who commit capital and openly compete with one another for investors' buy and sell orders

Electronic Communication Networks (ECN)

Trading systems which bring additional customer orders into Nasdaq

ECNs

Electronic communication networks (ECNs) are private trading networks that provide Market Makers and institutions with an anonymous way to enter orders for a stock into the marketplace.

Instinet is an example of ECN. Instinet allows premarket and postmarket trading, which is trading before the opening bell at 9:30am and after the bell at 4:00pm.

ECN quotes are posted on the Nasdaq Workstation II the same way Market Makers post their quotes.

Advantages of Being an ECN

Rather than risking their own capital to execute orders. **ECNs can simply match bids and asks**, and collect commissions.

The Advantages of ECNs
1. No Market Impact - Simply Match of Orders
2. Lower Commissions
3. Faster Trades
4. After-Hours Trading

ECNs Now Account for 30% of NASDAQ Trades and 5% of NYSE Trades

Largest Players
Instinet, Island, REDIBook

ECNs
Percent of NASDAQ Trading

Instinet	9.4%
Island	7.8%
Redibook	1.4%
Archipelago	1.4%
TradeBook	1.3%
Brass	1.0%
Strike	0.3%
Nextrade	0.3%
Attain	0.3%

SEC Study of Order Execution

U.S. Securities and
Exchange Commission

- Comparison of Order Execution on NYSE and NASDAQ

- Assessed Order Execution Spreads as well as Timing

- Measured Spreads and Timing of Individual Trades Using Matched Sample and Regression for Stocks in Different Market Cap Ranges

SEC Study of Order Execution

- The Effective Spread Measures the Execution Cost Paid by the Investor

- Measured as the 2* (Execution Price – the Midpoint of the Quoted Spread When the Order Arrived for Execution). It is Doubled to Make the Effective Spreads Look Like Quoted Spreads

- For Example: a Buy Order Arrives When the Quoted Spread is 20.25 – 19.75 and is Executed @20.125. The Effective Spread is 2 * (20.125 – 20) = $.25.

SEC Study of Order Execution

THE DIFFERENCE A MARKET MAKES

How the 'effective' spread, or the difference between the actual price an investor gets and the midpoint between the posted bid and ask prices for different size stocks, varies on the Nasdaq Stock Market and on the NYSE.*

Small
Market capitalization
of less than $200 million
8.3¢
16.4¢

Medium
Market capitalization
of $200 million to $1 billion
9.3¢
28.6¢

Large
Market capitalization
of more than $1 billion
9.3¢
15.8¢

Very Large
Includes stocks identified by Nasdaq
as very large for inclusion in report
8.3¢
7.1¢

NYSE
Nasdaq

*For market orders of 100 to 499 shares
Source: SEC

How the Market Works

Measures of the Stock Market

◆ **The Dow Jones Industrials Average (DJIA)**
  – 30 Stocks
  – Price–Weighted Index (Divisor)

◆ **The S&P 500**
  – 500 Stocks
  – Market–Value Weighted

◆ **Others**
  – NYSE, AMEX & NASDAQ
  – Russell 2000 and Wilshire 5000

Measures of the Stock Market

DowJones
Indexes

3M Company
Alcoa Incorporated
Altria Group, Incorporated
American Express Company
AT&T Corporation
Boeing Company
Caterpillar Incorporated
Citigroup Incorporated
Coca-Cola Company
DuPont

Eastman Kodak Company
Exxon Mobil Corporation
General Electric Company
General Motors Corporation
Hewlett-Packard Company
Home Depot Incorporated
Honeywell International Inc.
Intel Corporation
International Business Machines
International Paper Company

J.P. Morgan Chase & Company
Johnson & Johnson
McDonald's Corporation
Merck & Company, Incorporated
Microsoft Corporation
Procter & Gamble Company
SBC Communications Incorporated
United Technologies Corporation
Wal-Mart Stores Incorporated
Walt Disney Company

Measures of the Stock Market

Standard & Poors

▼ Desc	GICS®[1]	NC[2]	MKTCAP[3,4]	Level[5]	Daily	MTD	QTD	YTD
					(DD-MMM-YYYY)			
S&P 500		500	10,562,117	1,140.995	(0.27%)	0.87%	2.62%	2.62%
Energy	10	23	625,317	234.809	0.94%	3.47%	4.76%	4.76%
Materials	15	33	309,046	163.367	0.16%	3.81%	(1.19%)	(1.19%)
Industrials	20	59	1,135,215	251.992	(0.04%)	(0.17%)	0.90%	0.90%
Consumer Discretionary	25	87	1,162,968	249.099	(0.74%)	0.99%	0.16%	0.16%
Consumer Staples	30	37	1,194,265	236.293	0.66%	5.63%	5.72%	5.72%
Health Care	35	47	1,418,597	361.674	(0.43%)	0.70%	3.44%	3.44%
Financials	40	83	2,231,613	399.196	(0.01%)	2.09%	5.10%	5.10%
Information Technology	45	83	1,814,695	320.889	(1.48%)	(3.89%)	(0.55%)	(0.55%)
Telecommunications Services	50	12	373,327	117.018	(0.22%)	1.38%	5.12%	5.12%
Utilities	55	36	297,075	120.08	0.22%	(0.41%)	1.43%	1.43%

Measures of the Stock Market

STANDARD & POOR'S

Company	Mkt Cap ($ mil)	Index Weight	Sector Weight	GICS® Sector
General Electric	311,065.8	3.02%	27.75%	Industrials
Microsoft Corp.	297,775.4	2.89%	16.32%	Information Technology
Exxon Mobil Corp.	271,001.8	2.63%	45.42%	Energy
Pfizer, Inc.	269,621.7	2.62%	19.69%	Health Care
Citigroup Inc.	250,403.2	2.43%	11.79%	Financials
Wal-Mart Stores	229,588.8	2.23%	20.32%	Consumer Staples
Intel Corp.	210,330.4	2.04%	11.53%	Information Technology
American Int'l. Group	172,854.7	1.68%	8.14%	Financials
Cisco Systems	167,682.1	1.63%	9.19%	Information Technology
International Bus. Machines	159,448.8	1.55%	8.74%	Information Technology

Stock Market Measures

DJIA
S&P 500
Russell 2000
NASDAQ

The Market for Common Stock

◆ **Commissions**
  - **Retail**
  - **Discount**
  - **Institutional**

◆ **Daily Volume**

◆ **Market Share of Exchanges & OTC**

Average NYSE Daily Trading Volume

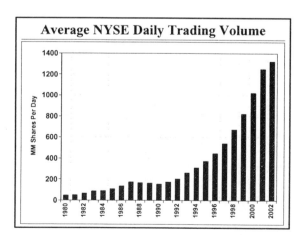

Market Shares for Exchanges

Market Share

By Trading
Volume

NASDAQ
54%

NYSE
45%

AMEX
1%

By Dollar
Volume

NASDAQ
44%

AMEX
1%

NYSE
55%

Stock Brokers

Full Service Brokers
Provide Personal Investment
Consulting Services

Discount Brokers
Execute Trades

Online Brokers
 Execute Trades Online

The Secondary Securities Markets
Recent Issues

NYSE Governance

Specialists Versus
Market-Makers

Round-the-Clock Trading

Competition Between NYSE,
OTC/AMEX, and ECNs and
Market Structure

Search for Best Price

Globalization of Financial Markets

- Technological Change and Deregulation Blur Distinctions Between Domestic and Foreign Markets

- Competition Lead to Further Deregulation

- Competition Lead to Financial Innovation Offering Opportunities In Value Creation

The Financial System, Intermediation, and Financial Institutions

The Financial System, Intermediation, and Financial Institutions

---

The Financial System, Intermediation, and Financial Institutions

This module introduces and defines financial intermediaries, and explores the economic role of such institutions. Objectives for this module include:

(1) Understanding the functions of the financial system and the <u>need for financial intermediaries</u> in this system
(2) Explaining the <u>different forms of financial intermediation</u> and how these are exploited by financial institutions;
(3) Provide an evaluation of the <u>different types of financial institutions</u>
(4) Explore the <u>Convergence of Financial Services</u>; and
(5) Discuss <u>Mutual Funds</u> as Financial Intermediaries

Financial Facts of the Day

The Largest Financial Institutions in the World

Bank Insurance Brokerage

Diversified Financial

Financial Intermediation and Financial Institutions

1. Financial Intermediation

2. Financial Institutions:
   Balance Sheet/Income Statement

3. Financial Institutions:
   Winning Strategies in the 1990s

4. The Convergence of Financial
   Services

Financial Intermediation

Willie Sutton
Famous Bank Robber

Question
Why do You
Rob Banks?

Depository Institutions and Securities Markets as Financial Intermediaries

RISING FORCE OF MARKETS
Share of total net credit market lending
75%

Depository
institutions*

50

25

Securities
markets

0
1960'65 '70 '75 '80 '85 '90 '95

*Depository institutions include
commercial banks and other institutional
lenders.
Note: Other sources include insurers,
pension funds, etc.
Sources: Federal Reserve Board Flow of Funds;
Mark Zandi, RFA Dismal Sciences

•There Has Been An
Increase In the Popularity
of Securities Markets In
Providing Financing For
Corporations

•Funds Provided By
Commercial Banks and
Other Institutional
Lenders Are On a Decline

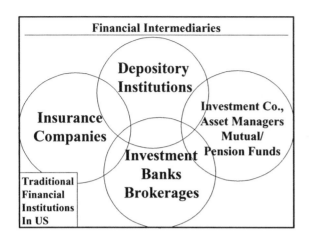

Financial Intermediaries

- Depository Institutions
- Insurance Companies
- Investment Co., Asset Managers Mutual/ Pension Funds
- Investment Banks Brokerages
- Traditional Financial Institutions In US

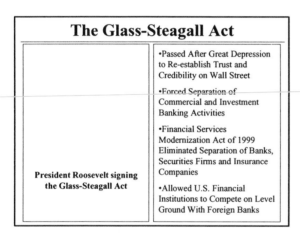

The Glass-Steagall Act

President Roosevelt signing the Glass-Steagall Act

- Passed After Great Depression to Re-establish Trust and Credibility on Wall Street
- Forced Separation of Commercial and Investment Banking Activities
- Financial Services Modernization Act of 1999 Eliminated Separation of Banks, Securities Firms and Insurance Companies
- Allowed U.S. Financial Institutions to Compete on Level Ground With Foreign Banks

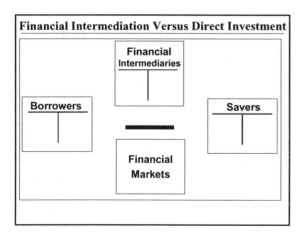

Financial Intermediation Versus Direct Investment

- Financial Intermediaries
- Borrowers
- Savers
- Financial Markets

Financial Institutions
Forms of Financial Intermediation

→ Denomination

→ Liquidity and Maturity

→ Default Risk/
Diversification

→ Economies of Scale in
Information and
Transactions Costs

_____

_____

_____

_____

_____

_____

_____

Denomination Intermediation

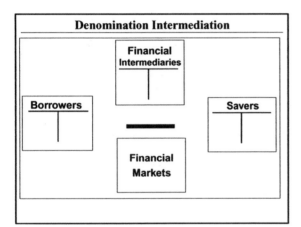

_____

_____

_____

_____

_____

_____

_____

Liquidity/Maturity Intermediation

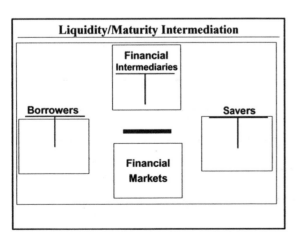

_____

_____

_____

_____

_____

_____

_____

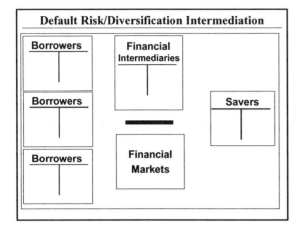

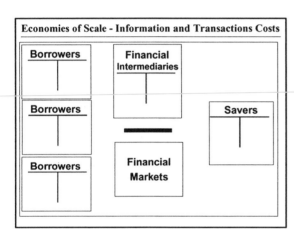

Financial Institutions
Forms of Financial Intermediation

→ **Denomination**

→ **Liquidity and Maturity**

→ **Default Risk/ Diversification**

→ **Economies of Scale in Information and Transactions Costs**

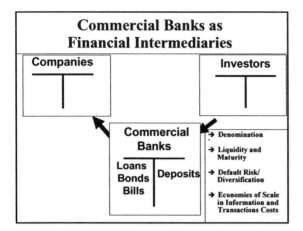

Commercial Banks as Financial Intermediaries

Companies

Investors

Commercial Banks

Loans
Bonds
Bills

Deposits

→ Denomination

→ Liquidity and Maturity

→ Default Risk/ Diversification

→ Economies of Scale in Information and Transactions Costs

Financial Institutions
Sources and Uses of Funds

Banks		Investment Banks	
Loans	Deposits	Securities	Debt

Insurance		Investment Co.	
Bonds	Reserves	Securities	Shares

Commercial Banks

Bank of America

JP Morgan Chase

HSBC

Wells Fargo

UBS

Deutsche Bank

```
┌─────────────────────────────────────┐
│          Investment Banks           │
├─────────────────────────────────────┤
│ Morgan Stanley Dean Witter          │
│                                     │
│        Merrill Lynch    Be Bullish  │
│   Goldman                           │
│   Sachs                             │
│              Charles Schwab         │
│                                     │
│   Lehman Brothers                   │
│                                     │
└─────────────────────────────────────┘
```

_____

_____

_____

_____

_____

_____

_____

```
┌─────────────────────────────────────┐
│         Insurance Companies         │
├─────────────────────────────────────┤
│  AIG                                │
│          BERKSHIRE HATHAWAY INC.    │
│                                     │
│  Alliance                  ING      │
│                                     │
│                                     │
│  OUI                                │
│  Paris AXA          Credit Group    │
│  2008               Suisse          │
│                                     │
└─────────────────────────────────────┘
```

_____

_____

_____

_____

_____

_____

_____

```
┌─────────────────────────────────────┐
│        Investment Companies         │
├─────────────────────────────────────┤
│   Fidelity Investments              │
│            The Vanguard Group       │
│                                     │
│   American Funds                    │
│                                     │
│            Franklin Templeton       │
│                                     │
│  Washington Mutual, Inc.            │
│              INVESCO                │
└─────────────────────────────────────┘
```

_____

_____

_____

_____

_____

_____

_____

Financial Institutions: Winning Strategies

What Strategies Led to The Big Increases in Market Capitalization for Financial Institutions?

Financial Institutions: Winning Strategies

Investment

Strageties

The Convergence of Financial Services

Deregulation -
   The Financial Services
   Modernization Act of 1999

Financial Innovation

Globalization and Integration
of Markets

Demographics

Information and
Telecommunications Technologies

Consumer Preferences

citigroup ☂

$700B in Assets, 100M Customers in 100 Countries, 170,000 Employees

CITIBANK⊕

1997 Net Profit - $4.5B

- ■ Life Insurance
- ■ Consumer Finance
- ■ Property Casualty Insurance
- ☒ Salomon Smith Barney

Travelers Group

1997 Net Profit - $3.4B

- ■ Emerging Mkts. In Consumer Bus.
- ■ Developed Mkts
- ■ Emerging Mkts in Corporate Bus.
- ☒ Global Rel. Banking

Banking, Insurance, Brokerage, Mutual Funds

Citigroup Companies:

- * Primerica PRIMERICA☂
- * Citibank citibank
- * Travelers Bank & Trust
- * Travelers Life & Annuity **Travelers**☂
- * Travelers Property Casualty
- * Salomon Smith Barney SALOMON SMITH BARNEY
- * Citigroup Asset Management citigroup☂
- * CitiFinancial citi financial
- * Associates
    - •On November 30th, 2000, Citigroup officially acquired The Associates

Commercial Banking
Investment Banking and Brokerage
Insurance
Asset Management – Mutual Funds

Time Value of Money

Chapter 8:
The Time Value of Money

Woolridge & Gray

Time Value of Money: Compounding and Discounting

Chapter Overview

- **8.1 Compounding and Future Value**

- **8.2 Present Value and Discounting**

- **8.3 Summary**

Compounding and Future Value: Topics to be Examined

How a single investment and multiple investments grow by compounding;

Changing the Compounding Period;

How taxes affect future values on your investments;

Finding Rates of Return.

Time Value of Money: Compounding and Discounting

- <u>Compounding</u>-going from a known value today, to an expected but unknown value in the future. Compounding-multiply, over a number of time periods, by number greater than 1.0.

- <u>Future value</u>-amount of money an investment will grow to by earning a certain rate of return over time.

Future Value and Compounding: How are they used in Practice?

Estimating your portfolio's future value at the time of your retirement.

Saving funds necessary to finance your child's education.

Estimating a corporation's yearly budget to fund pension payment requirements.

The Cost of Smoking—Money Blown Away

You quit your pack a day habit and invest your savings in a stock mutual fund

How much will you have at age 65?

Assume your current age is 20

Cost per pack is $3

Estimated rate of return is 12% a year

At 65, you expect to have......

<u>$1,487,262</u>

Types of Interest Payments

Simple Interest-interest to be paid only on the original principal invested. The interest is not reinvested. No interest is earned on interest.

Compound Interest-accumulating interest on an investment for more than one period and reinvesting the interest. Interest is earned on interest.

How a Single Investment Grows: Simple Interest

Year	Beginning Balance	Interest Earned	Ending Balance
1	$100.00	$8.00	$108.00
2	$108.00	$8.00	$116.00
3	$116.00	$8.00	$124.00

How a Single Investment Grows: Compound Interest

Year	Beginning Balance	Interest Earned	Ending Balance
1	$100.00	$8.00	$108.00
2	$108.00	$8.64	$116.64
3	$116.64	$9.33	$125.97

How a Single Investment Grows: Compound Interest

Year	Beginning Balance	Interest Earned	Ending Balance
1	$100.00	$8.00	$108.00
2	$108.00	$8.64	$116.64
3	$116.64	$9.33	$125.97

$100 * 1.08 ^ 1 = $108.00

$100 * 1.08 ^ 2 = $116.64

$100 * 1.08 ^ 3 = $125.97

Types of Problems for Single Payment Investments

Future Value of a Single Payment

Calculate the Rate of Return on a Single Payment

Calculate the Initial Payment Needed to have a Required Future Value

---

FV Formula for a Single Payment with Compound Interest

FV = PV * FVSP Factor (r,n)

FV = PV * (1.0 + r)^n

If PV = $100, r = 10%, n = 20 years, then:

FV = $100 * (1.10)^20

FV = $100 * (6.7275) = $672.75

Table 8-3 (Page 8-6) show FVSP info.

Future Value of a Single Payment Investment Using a Financial Calculator

- The five financial function keys, n—number of periods, r or i—interest rate or yield, PV—present value, PMT—periodic payment, and FV—future value
- Example: Nancy wants to invest $5000 today with a bank that promises to pay her 5% per year for 30 years

- Clear your calculator! Inputs are: n = 30, i = 5, PMT = 0, PV = -$5000—the cash outflow, solve for FV, which is equal to $21,609.71

Finding the rate of return on a single payment-FVSP Table 8-3

You invest $125 today

You have $314.77 in 12 years

Find your required rate of return

FV = PV * FVSP Factor (r,n)

$314.77 = $125 * (1+r)^12

(1+r)^12 = 314.77 / 125 = 2.5182

Find the 12-year factor in the Single Payment Table (8-3) closest to 2.5182

It is the 8% factor

Rate of Return on a Single Payment Investment (Calculator)

- Calculate the rate of return on a single investment.

- Thirty years ago, Nancy invested $5000. The investment has grown to $21,609.71. What is Nancy's rate of return?

- Clear your calculator! Inputs are: n = 30, FV = $21,609.71, PMT = 0, PV = -$5000—the cash outflow, solve for i, which is equal to 5%

Finding the initial investment for a Future Value (FVSP Table 8-3)

You need to invest _?_ Today @ 8% to have $314.77 in 12 years?

Find your required initial investment

FV = PV * FVSP Factor (5,12)

$314.77 = PV * 2.5182

PV = 314.77 / 2.5182 = <u>$125</u>

Calculate the Present Value Payment for a Future Value (Calculator)

- Calculate the initial payment that you need to receive an amount in the future.

- How much should Nancy deposit today at 5% to receive a compounded amount of $21,609.71 in 30 years.

- Inputs are: n = 30, FV = $21,609.71, PMT = 0, r = 5%, solve for PV, which is equal to -$<u>4,999.99.</u>

The Rule of 72 (for single payments)

How long it takes an investment to double in value for a given interest rate. Divide 72 by the interest rate to get the number of years. Not exact.

8%	72 / 8 = 9 years	$1.08 \wedge 9 = 1.999$
6%	72 / 6 = 12 years	$1.06 \wedge 12 = 2.012$
10%	72 / 10 = 7.2 years	$1.10 \wedge 7.2 = 1.986$

The Compounding Period: How it Affects Future Value

Shortening the compounding period increases the <u>Effective Annual Rate</u>

Annual @ 12% = $100*1.12 = $112.00

Semi-annual @ 6% = $100*1.06^2 = $112.36

Quarterly @ 3% = $100*1.03^4 = $112.55

Monthly @ 1% =$100*1.01^12 = $112.68

More frequent compounding is good for investors—higher effective annual rate.

The Effect of Taxes

Interest earned is usually taxable

Suppose your tax rate is 25% and you invest $100 at 8%

Investment	Interest Earned	Taxes	After-taxes
$100	$8	$2	$6

Your after-tax rate of return is 6%

After-tax rate=Before-tax rate*(1-tax rate)=8% * (1-.25)=6%

An Example of Compounding after Taxes

You invest $250 at 10%

Your tax rate is 40%

How much will you have in 25 years?

After-tax rate = 10% * (1-.40) = 6%

$250 * (1.06 ^ 25) = $1,073

Note that if you didn't pay taxes, you would have....

$250 * (1.10 ^ 25) = $2,709

Tax -advantaged investing for retirement

401(k) plans....named for paragraph 401(k) of the internal revenue code

Traditional I.R.A. (Individual Retirement Account)

Roth I.R.A.

FV Formula for Multiple Payments with Compound Interest

FV = Payment * FVMP Factor (r,n)

If Payment = $100/year, r = 10%, n = 20 years, then:

FV = $100 * FVMP Factor (10%, 20)

FV = $100 * (57.2750) = $5,727.50

Table 8-4 (Page 8-8) show FVMP info.

Types of Problems for Multiple Payment Investments

Future Value of Multiple Payments

Calculate the Rate of Return on Multiple Payments

Calculate the Multiple Payments Needed to have a Required Future Value

Future Value of Multiple Payments

What's the Future Value of investing $1 at the end of each year for four years?

10/27/2002	$1	$1 * 1.08^3 = 1.2597
10/27/2003	$1	$1 * 1.08^2 = 1.1664
10/27/2004	$1	$1 * 1.08^1 = 1.0800
10/27/2004	$1	$1 * 1.08^0 = <u>1.0000</u>
The sum of these is		**<u>4.5061</u>**

Check your FVMP table (Page 8-8) at 8%-4 years to see this number

---

Future Value of Multiple Payments: Practice Problem-no Taxes (Table 8-4)

Your plan is to invest $1,000 a year in a Roth IRA

You expect to earn 10% a year. How much will you have at age 65 if you begin at age 45?

$1,000 * 57.2750 = $57,275

Future Value of Multiple Payments: Practice Problem-with Taxes

Your plan is to invest $1,000 a year in a savings account

You expect to earn 10% a year but you will pay income taxes annually at the rate of 40%. How much will you have at age 65 if you begin at age 45?

$1,000 * 36.7856 = $36,785.60

Future Value of Multiple Payments Using a Financial Calculator

Nancy wants to invest $5,000 at the end of <u>every year</u> @ 5% per year for 30 years. What is the future value of her investment?

Clear your calculator! Inputs are: n = 30, i = 5, PV = 0, PMT = -$5000 the cash outflows, solve for FV, which equals <u>$332,194.23.</u>

Finding the Rate of return on a Multiple Payment Investments (Table 8-4)`

You invest $125 a year for 10 years
You end up with $2,150
Find your rate of return
$125 * Factor = $2,150
Factor = $2,150 / $125 = 17.2
Look across from 10 years till you find this factor

Answer: Between 10% and 12%

Finding the Rate of Return on a Multiple Payment Investments (Calculator)

You invest $125 a year for 10 years and end up with $2,150. Find your rate of return

Calculator inputs: PMT = -$125, PV = 0, n = 10, FV = $2,150, find i;

Rate of Return i = <u>11.58%</u>

Time Value of Money: Compounding and Discounting

- The math underlying discounting and the calculation of present value (*PV*) is the exact flip side to compounding and future value

- Present value is the mirror image of future value and discounting is the opposite of compounding

- <u>Discounting</u> is the process of going from an expected future value to a present value

- Discounting also means to multiply by a number less than 1.0, over a number of time periods

---

Time Value of Money: Compounding and Discounting

- <u>Present value</u> is the current value of expected future cash flows discounted at the appropriate discount rate.

- The <u>discount rate</u> is the interest rate used to calculate the present value of a future cash payment

- The <u>present value equation</u> for discounting a one-time cash flow for one period is equal to:

  $$PV = FV / (1.0 + r)$$

- The <u>PV Discount Factor</u> (r,n) for finding the present value of a payment to be received in *n* periods, discounted at *r* rate is:

  $$PVDF (r,n) = 1/(1 + r)^n$$

Why bother with Present Value?

PV is used to calculate loan payments and lease payments

PV is used by investors to estimate the value of bonds and stock

PV is used by corporations to make major investment decisions

144

Types of Problems for Single Investments

Present Value of a Single Payment

Calculate the Rate of Return on a Single Payment

Calculate the Initial Payment Needed to have a Required Future Value

---

Present Value Formula for a Single Payment (Table 8-6)

PV = Future Value * $[1/(1.0 + r)]^t$

If Future Value = $100, r = interest rate = 10%, t = time = 20 years, then:

PV = $100 * $[1/(1.10)]^{20}$

PVSP Factor (10%, 20 years) = 0.1486 (see Table 8-6).

PV = $100 * (.1486) = $14.86

Present Value of a Future Single Payment Investment Using a Financial Calculator

- **The five financial function keys are labeled, n—number of periods, r or i—interest rate or yield, PV—present value, PMT—payment, and FV—future value**
- **Example: Nancy wants to receive a lump sum of $100,000 in 30 years when she retires. If a bank that promises to pay her 8% per year, what amount does she need to deposit today?**
- **Clear your calculator! Inputs are: n = 30, i = 8, PMT = 0, FV = $100,000, solve for PV, which is equal to $9,937.73**
- **Check answer with Table 8-6.**

Finding the rate of return on a single payment-PVSP Table 8-6

You invest $125 today

You have $314.77 in 12 years

Find your required rate of return

PV = FV * PVSP Factor (r,n)

$125 = $314.77 * 1/(1+r)^12

1/(1+r)^12 = 125/314.77 = 0.3971

Find the 12-year factor in the Single Payment Table (8-6) closest to 0.3971

It is the 8% factor

Rate of Return on a Single Payment Investment (Calculator)

- Calculate the rate of return that we receive on an investment.

- Thirty years ago, Latisha invested $5000 with a bank. That investment has grown to $21,609.71. What was the rate of return on her single investment?

- Clear your calculator! Inputs are: n = 30, FV = $21,609.71, PMT = 0, PV = -$5000—the cash outflow, solve for i, which is equal to 5%

Finding the initial investment for a Future Value (FVSP Table 8-3)

You need to invest ? Today @ 8% to have $314.77 in 12 years?

Find your required initial investment

FV = PV * FVSP Factor (8,12)

$314.77 = PV * 2.5182

PV = 314.77 / 2.5182 = $125

Calculate the Present Value Payment for a Future Value (Calculator)

- Calculate the initial payment that need to make in order receive an amount in the future.

- How much should Nancy deposit at 5% interest to have a compounded amount of $21,609.71 in 30 years?

- Inputs are: n = 30, FV = $21,609.71, PMT = 0, r = 5%, solve for PV, which is equal to -$4,999.99.

Present Value of a Single Payment How Much Must Be Invested Today

Your no-smoking campaign will leave you with $1,487,262 in 45 years

That assumes 12% a year

How much must you invest today to produce $1,487,262 in 45 years?

The Parallel Nature of Present Value and Future Value

The future value of $9,069 (in 45 years) is....
$9,069 * (1.12^45)=$1,487,262

The present value of that $1,487,262 is....
$1,487,262 /(1.12^45) = $9,069
PVSP (12%, 45) = .0061 (Table 8-6)

Interpreting Present Value

What is the PV of $1 to be received in 5 years discounted at 8%?

Answer: $1/1.08^5 = $0.6806

What does this mean?
68 cents grows to $1 in 5 years

What's the PV at 10%
$1/1.10^5= $0.6209----it's lower
See the PVSP Table 8-6

Practice with Single Payment Bonds

You own an IBM bond that promises you the single payment of $1,000 on October 30, 2013

You want to sell the bond and the interest rate is 8%

What price do you get?

$1,000* (1/ 1.08^10) = $463

What return can the buyer anticipate?

8%

Practice With Bonds

Suppose the interest rate jumps to 12%.... What price do you get?

$1,000 * (1/1.12^ 10) = $322......the value of your bond fell from $463 to $322 due to a rise in interest rates

As interest rates go up, existing bond prices go……..
DOWN!!

Finding the Rate of Return for a Single Investment (Table 8-6)

You invest $150 now and get $281.57 in 10 years

Find your annual rate of return!

$150 = $281.57*PV Factor (Single Payment)

PV Factor (Single Payment) = $150 / $281.57 = **.5327**

This 10-year factor is between 6% and 7% in Table 8-6.

_____
_____
_____
_____
_____
_____
_____

Finding the Rate of Return for a Single Investment (Calculator)

You invest $150 now and get $281.57 in 10 years

Find your annual rate of return!

-$150 = PV, $281.57 = FV, Pmt = 0, n = 10, r = ?

Plug the above numbers into the calculator and
r=6.499977

_____
_____
_____
_____
_____
_____
_____

An Annuity is a sequence of equal multiple payments

Examples include....
Car lease payments or loan payments
Home mortgage payments
Social security payments to a retiree (called a life annuity)
20 annual payments received when you win the lottery

_____
_____
_____
_____
_____
_____
_____

Calculating the PV of Multiple Payments Using 12%

3/ 15/ 2005	$1* (1/1.12^1) =	0.8929
3 /15/ 2006	$1* (1/1.12^2) =	0.7972
3 /15/ 2007	$1* (1/1.12^3) =	0.7118

PV of $1 a year for 3 years is…………….. 2.4019

Check this number in
Table 8-7

Interpreting the PV Table Entries

How much must you invest
today at 12% to be able to
spend $1 a year for 20 years?
$7.47 ($7.4694)

For 25 years?
$7.84 ($7.8431)

A Quick Exercise on the PV of an Annuity-calculator

You win $50,000 a year for 20 years in a lottery
Your local bank is offering 8% a year
What's the PV of your prize?

9.8181 * $50,000 = $490,905 **Table 8-7**

Pmt = -$50,000, FV = 0, n=20, r=8%, PV=$490,907
(calculator)

If you won $490,905 you could invest it at the bank
at 8% and withdraw $50,000/yr for 20 years

The Basic Idea Behind Loan Calculations

The PV of the payments on a loan equals the amount of the loan.

You want to borrow $10,000 at 10% and repay with 3 equal annual payments. How much are your payments?

$10,000 = 2.4869 * Payment

Payment = $10,000 / 2.4869 = $4,021

You repay 3 years * $4,021 = $12,063 so $2,063 is interest

An Amortization Table for this Loan

Year	Beginning Balance	Interest Owed	Payment	Principal Reduction
1	$10,000	$1,000	$4,021	$3,021
2	$6,979	$698	$4,021	$3,323
3	$3,656	$366	$4,021	$3,655

The beginning balance number is the amount you could pay to entirely payoff the loan at a point in time

---

Practice with a Home Mortgage

You borrow $100,000 at 8%

You will repay with 30 equal annual payments

How much are your payments?

$100,000 = 11.2578 * Payment

Payment = $100,000 / 11.2578 =   -$8,883 (Table 8-7)

PV = $100,000, n = 30, r = 8%, FV = 0, Pmt = -$8,882.74 (calculator)

The Mortgage Continued

You have an option to prepay your 30-year mortgage at anytime.

After the 10th year, how much do you owe?

$8,883 * 9.8181 = $87,214 [Table 8-7 (8%, 20)]

After the 20th year, how much do you owe?

$8,883 * 6.7101 = $59,606 [Table 8-7 (8%, 10)]

Finding the Rate of Return for an Annuity

You borrow $100,000 and repay the bank with 20 equal annual payments of $12,000
Find your Annual rate of Return

$100,000 = $12,000 * PV Annuity Factor

PV Annuity Factor = $100,000/$12,000= **8.3333** found between 10% and 12% in the PV multiple payments Table 8-7

$100,000 = PV, n = 20, Pmt = -$12,000, FV = 0, Solve for Annual Rate of Return: **r = 10.3156%**

Discounted Cash Flow Valuation

Chapter 9:
Discounted Cash Flow Valuation

Woolridge & Gray

Discounted Cash Flow Valuation

Chapter Objectives

- Learn to calculate future and present value of level cash flow streams and uneven cash flow streams

- Learn to calculate loan payments, effective interest rates, and amortization schedules

- Learn to value stocks and bonds using the DCF approach

Discounted Cash Flow Valuation

Chapter Overview

- 9.1 Introduction to DCF Valuation

- 9.2 Valuing Level Cash Flows

- 9.3 Valuing Uneven Cash Flows

- 9.4 Summary

Introduction to DCF Valuation

- DCF determines the *value* of an investment.
- The markets determine the *price* of an investment.
- You decide, based on price or cost, if the investment is undervalued, overvalued, or fairly-valued.
- Your buy/sell decision should be based solely on *price versus value*.

VALUE - WHAT AN INVESTMENT
SHOULD BE WORTH
THEN COMPARE THE PRICE
IT IS SELLING AT & MAKE
THE DECISION BASED ON THIS

PRICE TOO HIGH = DON'T BUY

Introduction to DCF Valuation-Definitions

- The *value* of an investment (stock, bond, mortgage, etc.) equals the present value of its expected cash flows, discounted (reduced) for their risk and timing.

- *Expected cash flows* are the most likely cash payments (dividends, interest, capital gain or loss) that you can expect (not hope) to receive.

Introduction to DCF Valuation-Definitions

- *Discount:* multiply a number by less than one.
- *Discount rate*: a function of time and risk: discount rate = f (time, risk)
- *Discount factor:* a function of both time and the discount rate- [discount factor = f (time, discount rate)]
- *Present value (PV)* of an investment is the sum of the expected cash flows multiplied by their respective discount factors

DISCOUNT FACTOR DECREASING
WHEN TIME INCREASING OR
INTEREST RATE INCREASES

Introduction to DCF Valuation: Loans

- *Level cash flows*: the interest rate and cash flows associated with the loans, mortgages, and annuities are fixed and do not change;

- A *loan* is an obligation under which a person borrows money from a lender;

- *Terms* of the loan state an interest rate and a repayment or *amortization schedule*.

Introduction to DCF Valuation: Mortgages

- Home mortgage: an obligation under which a person borrows money from a bank and uses the proceeds to purchase a house or condominium.

- Amortization schedule: Level payments over a long time period, usually 20 to 30 years.

TYPICALLY HOME MORTGAGES
HAVE LOWER INTEREST
RATES & LONGER
AMORTIZATION SCHEDULE

Introduction to DCF Valuation: Annuities

- An *life annuity* is contract sold by pension funds and life insurance companies;

- Pays a specified amount of money per year to owner;

- Amortization schedule more complex than loans or mortgage.

- Investor makes a single payment or multiple payments then withdraws funds upon her retirement.

Introduction to DCF Valuation: Mortgage Example- (Table 8-7)

- Gary borrows $100,000 from a bank at 8% and 25 year mortgage. What is his annual payment?
  - n = 25 years, PV = $100,000, r or i = 8%, FV = 0
  - PV = PMT * PVMP Factor (25, 8%)
  - $100,000 = PMT * 10.6748
  - $100,000/10.6748 = PMT
  - PMT = -$9,368/year
  - Total Payments = 25 * -$9,368 = -$234,197
  - Interest = -$134,197, Principal Repayment = -$100,000

Introduction to DCF Valuation: Mortgage Example-Rates up 2% to 10%

- Interest rates on mortgages increase by 2% to 10%, what is Gary's annual payment?
  - n = 25 years, PV = $ 100,000, r or i = 10%, FV = 0
  - PV = PMT * PVMP Factor (25, 10%)
  - $100,000 = PMT * 9.0770
  - $100,000/9.0770 = PMT
  - PMT = -$10,608/year   11,016
  - Total Payments = 25 * -$10,608 = $265,200
  - Interest = -$165,200, Principal Repayment = -$100,000

Introduction to DCF Valuation: Mortgage Example-Rates drop 2% to 6%

- If interest rates on mortgages decrease by 2% to 6%, what is Gary's annual payment?
  - n = 25 years, PV = $ 100,000, r or i = 6%, FV = 0
  - PV = PMT * PVMP Factor (25, 6%)
  - $100,000 = PMT * 12.7834
  - $100,000/12.7834 = PMT
  - PMT = -$7,823/year
  - Total Payments = 25 * -$7,823 = $195,567
  - Interest = -$95,567, Principal Repayment = -$100,000

Introduction to DCF Valuation: The Three-Step Approach

1. Develop a set of *expected cash flows*;
2. Estimate the *discount rate* and calculate the discount factors;
3. Multiply the cash flows by the discount factors and add them to determine the *value* of the asset.

Decision Rule:
- **If the *value* of an asset is *greater* than its *price*—Buy it!**
- **If the *value* is *less* than its *price*—Sell it!**

Valuing Level Cash Flows: Amortizing a loan

- **Example: Randy likes fast women and expensive cars. He wants to buy a BMW for $50,000? He can finance it with a bank loan at 10% for 4 years. His annual payment is $15,774. What is his <u>amortization schedule</u>?**

| | | | | | Interest Rate | | 10.00% |
| | | | | | Discount Rate | | 10.00% |
Year	Beginning Principal	Interest Payment	Principal Payment	Annual Payment	Discount Factor	DCF	Ending Principal
1	$50,000	$5,000	$10,774	$15,774	0.9091	$14,340	$39,226
2	$39,226	$3,923	$11,851	$15,774	0.8264	$13,036	$27,375
3	$27,375	$2,737	$13,037	$15,774	0.7513	$11,851	$14,338
4	$14,338	$1,434	$14,340	$15,774	0.683	$10,774	
Totals		$13,094	$50,002	$63,096		$50,001	

Valuing Level Cash Flows- Spreadsheet

- **An Excel Spreadsheet makes the DCF calculation easy. Assume interest rates on similar car loans increase to 11%. What's Randy's loan now worth.**
- **Discount the cash flows now at 11%. Plug 11% into the discount rate slot and the DCF value of Randy's $50,000 car loan is $48,938.**

| | | | | | Interest Rate | | 10.00% |
| | | | | | Discount Rate | | 11.00% |
Year	Beginning Principal	Interest Payment	Principal Payment	Annual Payment	Discount Factor	DCF	Ending Principal
1	$50,000	$5,000	$10,774	$15,774	0.9009	$14,211	$39,226
2	$39,226	$3,923	$11,851	$15,774	0.8116	$12,803	$27,375
3	$27,375	$2,737	$13,037	$15,774	0.7312	$11,534	$14,338
4	$14,338	$1,434	$14,340	$15,774	0.6587	$10,391	
Totals		$13,094	$50,002	$63,096		$48,938	

WHEN INTEREST RATES INCREASE/DECREASE THEIR IS AN INVERSE RELATIONSHIP WITH ALL FINANCIAL INVESTMENTS

Valuing Level Cash Flows- Calculator

- Using a financial calculator for PV: Five financial function keys: n—number of periods, r or i—interest rate or yield, PV—present value, PMT—payment, and FV—future value

- Randy's Car Loan—Valuing a four-year, 10% loan with a payment of -$15,773.54, discounted @ 11%.

- Inputs are: n = 4, i = 11, FV = 0, PMT = -$15,773.54, solve for PV, which is equal to $48,936.55

Valuing Uneven Cash Flows-Projects

- Most real world investments such as projects, stocks and bonds do not have a single cash flow or level expected cash flows.
- A *project* or venture is an investment to produce a product or provide a service that will generate money in the future.
- *Cash Inflows*- additional revenues coming into the company as a result of the project.
- *Cash Outflows*- additional expenses being spent by the company as a result of the project.

Valuing Uneven Cash Flows-Bonds

- A *bond* is a debt instrument. Corporations, the US Government, and municipalities issue bonds.

- Bonds are payable from taxes from US government or the general revenues of a corporation.

- *Cash inflows* to an investor are bond interest payments, usually every 6 months, and repayment of principal.

Valuing Uneven Cash Flows-Stocks

- A *stock* represents ownership interest in a corporation.

- The *cash inflows* consist of dividends and increase (or decrease) in stock price.

- There is no maturity associated with a stock—the life of a stock is infinite.

- The risk of a stock is hard to quantify, making it difficult to determine the proper discounting rate.

Valuing Uneven Cash Flows Using a Calculator

- Most popular financial calculators have their own specific systems for entering uneven sequential cash flows, and then discounting those cash flows at a uniform discount rate

- HP-12C model:
  - First input the number of periods and press the n button.
  - Then input the discounting rate and press the i button.
  - Then enter cash flow, press the blue *g* button, and press the *CFj* button. Use Nj button for equal cash flows.
  - Press the yellow *f* button and then press the *NPV* button to calculate the discounted present value for the cash flows

Valuing Uneven Cash Flows of a Project-Using a Spreadsheet

- Bill wants to invest in new machinery to increase paper production and revenues by $3,000,000 per year initially.

- Cost of pulp and additional raw material for the project is $2,500,000 per year. Additional O&M expense of the project will be $100,000 per year.

- Bill estimates revenues will increase at the rate of 6% per year and that costs will increase at a lower rate of 4% per year. The machinery is expected to last 8 years and have no salvage value at the end of this period.

- Projects of similar risk have a discounting rate of 14%.

- How much is this project worth?

9.3 Valuing Uneven Cash Flows Using a Spreadsheet — Lemont Paper Project

What do we know? N = 8 years, r = 14%, initial cash inflow is $3,000,000 and increases 6% per year, initial cash outflow is $2,600,00 and increases 4% per year.

			Discount Rate =		14%
Year	Cash Inflow	Cash Outflow	Net Cash Flow	Discount Factor	DCF
1	$3,000	($2,600)	$400	0.8772	$351
2	$3,180	($2,704)	$476	0.7695	$366
3	$3,371	($2,812)	$559	0.675	$377
4	$3,573	($2,925)	$648	0.5921	$384
5	$3,787	($3,042)	$746	0.5194	$387
6	$4,015	($3,163)	$851	0.4556	$388
7	$4,256	($3,290)	$966	0.3996	$386
8	$4,511	($3,421)	$1,089	0.3506	$382
Total			$5,735		$3,021

Valuing Uneven Cash Flows of a Bond Using a Spreadsheet

- Assume that the U.S. Government has issued a Bond with an 8% interest rate, five-years to the maturity of the Bond, and a principal payment of $1,000.
- The Bond pays interest in the amount of $40 dollars (equal to $1,000 * 8% * ½ year) two times per year (April 1 and October 1), plus the $1,000 repayment of the principal at maturity.
- Also assume that the interest rate associated with this type of bond has increased to 10% in today's market.
- What is the current value of this Bond?

Valuing Uneven Cash Flows of a Bond Using a Spreadsheet

	Semi Annual Rate =		5%
Period	Cash Flow	Discount Factor	DCF
1	40	0.9524	38.1
2	40	0.907	36.28
3	40	0.8638	34.55
4	40	0.8227	32.91
5	40	0.7835	31.34
6	40	0.7462	29.85
7	40	0.7107	28.43
8	40	0.6768	27.07
9	40	0.6446	25.78
10	1040	0.6139	638.47
Total	$1,400.00		$922.78

N = 10
PMT = 40
R = 5
FV = 1000
PV = ???

Valuing Uneven Cash Flows of a Stock Using a Spreadsheet

- **Valuing a stock involves the same analysis as valuing a fixed-rate mortgage loan, or the U.S. Government Bond.**
- **However, in estimating future cash flows there are two important exceptions:**
  - The Bond and the mortgage have *cash flows that are known with certainty*, while the range of future cash flows for a stock can be enormous.
  - Common stock represents ownership in a corporation, which has an *infinite life* unlike bonds and mortgages

---

ValuePro 2002 - [VP2002.BWB]
File Edit ValuePro Window Help

Valuation Date   10/24/2003

ValuePro 2002
General Input Screen
Intrinsic Stock Value $59.29
General Inputs

General Inputs			
Company Ticker...	ABC Corp		
Excess Return Period (years)	10	Depreciation Rate (% of Rev.)	7.20
Revenues ($mil)	10637	Investment Rate (% of Rev.)	20.60
Growth Rate (%)	13.00	Working Capital (% of Rev.)	-1.20
Net Operating Profit Margin (%)	28.00	Short-Term Assets ($mil)	0
Tax Rate (%)	31.10	Short-Term Liabilities($mil)	0
Stock Price($)	47.75	Equity Risk Premium (%)	3.00
Shares Outstanding (mil)	694.6	Company Beta	0.75
10-year Treasury Yield (%)	5.92	Value of Debt Out. ($mil)	4331
Bond Spread to Treasury (%)	1.00	Value of Pref. Stock Out. ($mil)	368
Preferred Stock Yield (%)	7.00	Company WACC (%)	7.73

ValuePro 2002 - [VP2002.BWB]
File Edit ValuePro Window Help

Valuation Date   10/24/2003

ValuePro 2002
General Pro Forma Screen
10-year Excess Return Period
ABC Corp

Disc. Excess Return Period FCFF	$6,527	Total Corporate Value	$46,469
Discounted Residual Value	$39,943	Less Debt	($4,931)
Short-Term Assets	$0.0	Less Preferred Stock	($368)
Total Corporate Value	$46,469	Less Short-Term Liabilities	$0
		Total Value to Common Equity	$41,180
		Intrinsic Stock Value	**$59.29**

(2)	(3)	(4)	(5)	(6)	(7)	(8)	(9)	(10)	(11)	(12)	(13)
12 Months Ending	Revenues	NCP	Adj. Taxes	NOPAT	Invest.	Deprec.	Change in Invest.	Change in Working Capital	FCFF	Discount Factor	Discounted FCFF
10/24/2003	10,687										
10/24/2004	12,076	3,140	976	2,163	2,488	869	1,618	-17	562	0.9293	521
10/24/2005	13,646	3,548	1,103	2,445	2,811	983	1,829	-19	635	0.8617	547
10/24/2006	15,420	4,009	1,247	2,762	3,177	1,110	2,066	-21	717	0.7999	574
10/24/2007	17,425	4,530	1,409	3,121	3,590	1,255	2,335	-24	811	0.7425	602
10/24/2008	19,690	5,119	1,592	3,527	4,056	1,418	2,638	-27	916	0.6892	631
10/24/2009	22,250	5,785	1,799	3,986	4,583	1,602	2,981	-31	1,035	0.6396	662
10/24/2010	25,142	6,537	2,033	4,504	5,179	1,810	3,369	-35	1,170	0.5936	695
10/24/2011	28,411	7,387	2,297	5,090	5,853	2,046	3,807	-39	1,322	0.5513	729
10/24/2012	32,104	8,347	2,596	5,751	6,613	2,312	4,302	44	1,454	0.5117	764
10/24/2013	36,278	9,432	2,933	6,499	7,473	2,612	4,861	-50	1,588	0.4750	802
	36,278	9,432	2,933	6,499	2,612	2,612	0	0	84,069	0.4750	39,343

Capital Budgeting and Measures of Investment Return-NPV, IRR and More

Chapter 10: Capital Budgeting and Measures of Investment Return

Woolridge & Gray

Capital Budgeting and Measures of Investment Return

Chapter Objectives

- Learn the process of capital budgeting and estimation of incremental cash costs and benefits

- Learn the standard techniques for measuring investment returns relating to capital budgeting problems

- Understand the contribution of capital budgeting towards increasing stock prices of a company and maximizing shareholder value

---

Capital Budgeting and Measures of Investment Return

Chapter Overview

- 10.1   Capital Budgeting
- 10.2   Net Present Value
- 10.3   Internal Rate of Return
- 10.4   Other Measures Relating to Capital Budgeting
    - Payback Period
    - Book Rate of Return
    - Profitability Index

Capital Budgeting and Measures of Investment Return

10.1 Capital Budgeting

- **Capital budgeting-process of planning and managing a firm's long-term investment in projects and ventures**
- **Capital Budgeting involves estimating the** *amount, timing, and risk of future cash flows*
- **Capital budgeting:**
  - starts with estimation of incremental cash flows from a project;
  - create a time line of expected cash flows; and
  - compare the present value of the cash flows with cost of project

---

Capital Budgeting and Measures of Investment Return

10.2 Net Present Value (NPV)

- **NPV of an investment-difference between the value and cost of investment.**

- **The value of any project is equal to the present value of its expected cash flows, discounted for risk and timing.**

- NPV Rule-invest in projects if NPV is positive. Reject if NPV is negative

---

Capital Budgeting and Measures of Investment Return

Net Present Value Example

Textile Inc is considering buying a new machine. The machine requires an initial outlay of $250,000 and is expected to generate incremental cash inflows of $120,000 for the next 5 years and requires $30,000 yearly cash outflows for maintenance. At the end of five years, the machine will have no disposable value. Calculate the Net Present Value of the project if the discount rate is 15% per year

Capital Budgeting and Measures of Investment Return

Procedure for solving the NPV Problem
1. Estimate cash flows from the new machine

Year	0	1	2	3	4	5
Inflows	-	120	120	120	120	120
Outflows	(250)	(30)	(30)	(30)	(30)	(30)
Net Cash Flows	(250)	90	90	90	90	90

Capital Budgeting and Measures of Investment Return

Procedure for solving the NPV Problem
2. Calculate the discounted cash flows

Year	0	1	2	3	4	5
Net	(250)	90	90	90	90	90
PV Factor (*)	1.000	0.870	0.756	0.658	0.572	0.497
Discounted Cash Flow	(250)	78.26	68.05	59.18	51.46	44.75

(*) PV Factor = $1/(1 + r)^t$

Capital Budgeting and Measures of Investment Return

Procedure for solving the NPV Problem
3. Calculate NPV and make the decision based on NPV Rule

Year	0	1	2	3	4	5
Discounted Cash Flow	(250)	78.26	68.05	59.18	51.46	44.75
NPV	51.69					
NPV is positive—Invest in the machine						

Capital Budgeting and Measures of Investment Return

10.3 Internal Rate of Return (IRR)

- IRR-rate of return expected to be earned on a project.

- IRR-discounting rate that makes the net present value of an investment equal to zero

- IRR Rule as an investment criterion:
    - if the investment has IRR that is higher than some pre-determined required rate of return, accept investment.
    - if the IRR is lower than required rate of return, reject.

Capital Budgeting and Measures of Investment Return

Internal Rate of Return Example

- Let us continue with the same example of Textile Inc.

    Textile Inc is considering buying a new machine for spinning. The machine requires an initial outlay of $250,000 and is expected to generate incremental cash inflows of $120,000 for the next 5 years and requires $30,000 yearly cash outflows for maintenance. At the end of five years, the machine will have no disposable value. Calculate the IRR of the project

---

Capital Budgeting and Measures of Investment Return

Procedure for solving the IRR
1. Estimate NPV from the machine based on a discount rate. In our case let us start with 15% per year

Year	0	1	2	3	4	5
Net Cash Flows	(250)	90	90	90	90	90
PV Factor	1.000	0.870	0.756	0.658	0.572	0.497
Discounted Cash Flow	(250)	78.26	68.05	59.18	51.46	44.75
NPV	51.69					

Capital Budgeting and Measures of Investment Return

Procedure for solving the IRR

2. Since the NPV calculated at step 1 is positive we increase the discount rate because IRR is the rate at which NPV of the project is 0. Now we take a discount rate of 25% per year

Year	0	1	2	3	4	5
Cash Flows	(250)	90	90	90	90	90
PV Factor	1.000	0.800	0.640	0.512	0.410	0.328
Discounted Cash Flow	(250)	72.00	57.60	46.08	36.86	29.49
NPV	(7.96)					

Capital Budgeting and Measures of Investment Return

Procedure for solving the IRR

3. We continue the process till we find the rate at which NPV is 0. In this example a discount rate of 23.44% gives an NPV of 0 and hence IRR is 23.44% per year

Year	0	1	2	3	4	5
Cash Flows	(250)	90	90	90	90	90
PV Factor	1.000	0.810	0.656	0.532	0.431	0.349
Discounted Cash Flow	(250)	72.91	59.07	47.85	38.76	31.40
NPV	0					

Capital Budgeting and Measures of Investment Return

Procedure for solving the IRR

4. We now compare the IRR calculated with a pre-determined required rate of return and apply the IRR rule to make the decision.

IRR of 23.44% is greater than the required rate of return of 15% per year—Invest in the new machine

Capital Budgeting and Measures of Investment Return

10.4   Other Measures – Payback Period

- Payback period-length of time for the return on an investment takes to cover the cost of the investment.
- Payback period-involves only gross cash flows and not discounted cash flows.
- Payback rule as an investment criterion:
  - accept the investment if its payback period is less than a predetermined number of years;
  - reject the investment if its payback period is greater than the predetermined number of years.

Capital Budgeting and Measures of Investment Return

Payback Period Example

- Tools Inc plans to invest in a new machinery that is expected to cost $100,000. The new machine will generate cash flows of $20,000 every year. Calculate the pay back period

Payback period = 100,000/20,000 = 5 years

If the company has a pre-determined payback period that is higher than the estimated payback period then accept the project, otherwise reject the project

---

Capital Budgeting and Measures of Investment Return

10.4   Other Measures – Book Rate of Return

- Book Rate of Return-an accounting ratio calculated by dividing the company's accounting profits by the book value of the company's assets.
- Book rate of return rule as an investment criterion:
  - accept the investment if its book rate of return exceeds a predetermined target book return;
  - reject the investment if its book rate of return is less than a target book return.

Capital Budgeting and Measures of Investment Return

Book Rate of Return Problem

Continuing with Tools Inc problem and given that Tools Inc. will depreciate the machine fully over the five year period. Calculate the book rate of return

Book Value (Beg)	Income	Book Rate of Return
100,000	20,000	20,000/100,000 = 20%
80,000	20,000	20,000/ 80,000 = 25%
60,000	20,000	20,000/ 60,000 = 33%
40,000	20,000	20,000/ 40,000 = 50%
20,000	20,000	20,000/ 20,000 = 100%

Capital Budgeting and Measures of Investment Return

10.4 Other Measures – Profitability Index (PI)

- PI- The NPV of an investment, divided by its cost.
- PI is used to identify projects that will receive the best return associated with the amount of dollars invested by ranking the projects by PI
- PI rule is:
  - accept the venture with the highest profitability index first;
  - then accept ventures with lower and lower positive PI's until the projects expend the capital budget;
  - do not accept projects with a negative PI.

Capital Budgeting and Measures of Investment Return

Profitability Index Problem

Calculate the profitability Index for the 3 projects given below:

Project	PV	Cost	NPV	Profitability Index
1	5,000	4,200	800	800/4,200 = 0.19
2	2,500	2,000	500	500/2,000 = 0.25
3	3,000	2,700	300	300/2,700 = 0.11

Based on Profitability Index Project 2 will be chosen first, followed by project 1 and then by project 3

The Ten Principles of Finance Relating to Valuation

Chapter 11: Ten Principles of Finance Relating to Valuation

Woolridge & Gray

The Ten Principles of Finance Relating to Valuation

Chapter Overview

- 11.1 Principle 1: Higher Returns Require Taking More Risk
- 11.2 Principle 2: Efficient Capital Markets are Tough to Beat
- 11.3 Principle 3: Rational Investors are Risk Averse
- 11.4 Principle 4: Supply and Demand Drive Stock Prices in the Short-run
- 11.5 Principle 5: When Analyzing Returns, Simple Averages are Never Simple

---

The Ten Principles of Finance Relating to Valuation

Chapter Overview

- 11.6 Principle 6: Transaction Costs, Taxes and Inflation are Your Enemies
- 11.7 Principle 7: Time and the Value of Money are Closely Related
- 11.8 Principle 8: Asset Allocation is a Very Important Decision
- 11.9 Principle 9: Asset Diversification Reduces Risk
- 11.10 Principle 10: An Asset Pricing Model Should be Used to Value Investments

The Ten Principles of Finance Relating to
Valuation

**11.1   Principle 1: Higher Returns Require Taking
More Risk**

- A trade-off exists between expected returns and risks on
an investment
- Safe investments have low returns
- High returns require investors to take big risks
- Ibbotson and Sinquefield study of historical annual rates
and distributions of returns on various classes of
investments from Treasury bills to stocks shows the
direct relationship between the expected return of an asset
and the risk associated with receiving that return

**The Ten Principles of Finance Relating to
Valuation**

11.1   Higher Returns Require Taking More Risk

The results of the Ibbotson and Sinquefield study is shown below:

	Return	Std Dev.
Treasury Bills	3.8%	3.2%
Government Bonds	5.3%	9.4%
Corporate Bonds	5.8%	8.6%
Large Company Stock	10.7%	20.2%
Small Company Stock	12.5%	33.2%

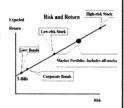

Probability of Reward versus Risk and Reversion to the Mean

Before you invest in an asset, you should assess whether the probabilities of reward or risk are equal or skewed.

Over time there is a tendency for returns and risk of asset markets to revert to average levels—reversion to the mean.

When stock prices are at relatively low levels by P/E ratios or P/BV ratios or P/S ratios, chances for a good return increase and the market is a *buy*.

When these ratios are at high levels, sell or avoid a buy.

Probability of Reward versus Risk and Reversion to the Mean

Over the long-run the returns associated with stocks have tracked their growth rate in earnings.

During the 1995-99 period the average return on the S&P 500 was 28.7%, and the average growth in earnings was under 10%.

During the late 90's prices of technology stocks were at levels that were much higher than their profits from operation could ever support.

Reversion to the mean suggests that the stock market run was unsustainable and much lower or negative returns were on the horizon to bring averages back into line with historic returns.

The Ten Principles of Finance Relating to Valuation

11.2 Principle 2: Efficient Capital Markets are Tough to Beat

- According to the theory of efficient capital markets (ECM): the stock market is brutally efficient; current stock prices reflect all publicly available information; and stock prices react completely, correctly, and almost instantaneously to incorporate the receipt of new information

- If the stock market is efficient, it would be useless to forecast future prices by technical analysis and fundamental analysis

What do we mean by Efficient Markets?

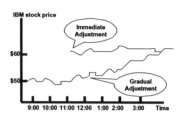

The Ten Principles of Finance Relating to Valuation

11.2 Efficient Capital Markets are Tough to Beat

- Various studies have been undertaken to test the notion of efficient capital markets and most of the studies have found results that were consistent with efficient capital markets
- However, Fama and French study found that stocks with a high book to market value ratio consistently outperformed stocks with low book to market ratios, p/e ratios and market capitalization considerations
- Even if some anomalies exist, capital markets are reasonably efficient and it is difficult for an investor to consistently beat the investment returns associated with a buy-and-hold strategy

Markets may not be all that efficient!

1992 Fama and French Stock Return Study Portfolios Based on Ascending Book Equity/Market Equity Ratios					
Portfolio	Monthly Return	Annualized Return	Avg. Number of Stocks	Weighted Avg. Return	Difference in Return
1A	0.30%	3.60%	89	14.99%	-11.39%
1B	0.67%	8.04%	98	14.99%	-6.95%
2	0.87%	10.44%	209	14.99%	-4.55%
3	0.97%	11.64%	222	14.99%	-3.35%
4	1.04%	12.48%	226	14.99%	-2.51%
5	1.17%	14.04%	230	14.99%	-0.95%
6	1.30%	15.60%	235	14.99%	0.61%
7	1.44%	17.28%	237	14.99%	2.29%
8	1.50%	18.00%	239	14.99%	3.01%
9	1.59%	19.08%	239	14.99%	4.09%
10A	1.92%	23.04%	120	14.99%	8.05%
10B	1.83%	21.96%	117	14.99%	6.97%
			2261		

F&F Study shows interesting anomaly

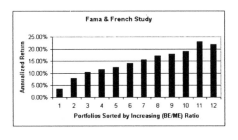

Fama & French Study

Annualized Return vs Portfolios Sorted by Increasing (BE/ME) Ratio

---

The Ten Principles of Finance Relating to Valuation

11.3 Principle 3: Rational Investors are Risk Averse

• Risk aversion means that a rational investor prefers less risk to more risk. "A bird in hand is worth two in the bush." "A safe dollar is worth more than a risky dollar."

• Finance theory is based upon the assumption that investors exhibit risk averse behavior

• A risk-averse investor does not avoid risk at all cost. He takes some small risks

• As an investor, it is important to determine your risk/return   profile and identify favorable investments before investing

---

Normal Distributions of Returns

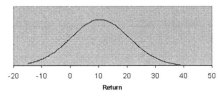

Normal Distribution with mean = 10.50% and standard deviation = 10.25%

Return

Return Distributions of Two Stocks

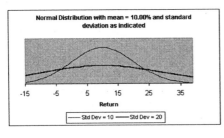

Normal Distribution with mean = 10.00% and standard deviation as indicated

Return

Std Dev = 10 — Std Dev = 20

Rational Investors are Risk Averse

Risk aversion is a good trait.

Realize what type of investor you are and how much risk you can stomach and afford

Investor personality quizzes Appendix 11-A

Carefully research your choices and make investments that you believe are undervalued and have a higher probability of increasing in value than decreasing

The Ten Principles of Finance Relating to Valuation

11.4 Principle 4: Supply and Demand Drive Stock Prices in the Short-run

- The market price of a stock is determined by the interaction of the supply of stock by sellers and the demand for stock by buyers

- In the short-run, a stock's current price may be heavily influenced by a very temporary and extreme supply and demand imbalance or by the stock market's reaction to the receipt of new information and may not have anything to do with the true long-term value of a company

The Ten Principles of Finance Relating to Valuation

11.4 Supply and Demand Drive Stock Prices in the Short-run

- Current price is where the supply of stock intersects with the demand for stock
- Lower commissions of 90's greatly increased demand for stocks thereby driving up prices
- If investor demand for a type of company exists, investment bankers will partner with entrepreneurs to create the companies to fill the demand
- Eventually, supply will catch up to demand and when that occurs, demand inevitably falls

---

Supply and Demand Drive Stock Prices in the Short-run

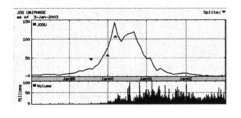

Supply and Demand Drive Stock Prices in the Short-run

A stock's current price * outstanding shares equals market equity.

VA Linux up 733%, FreeMarkets, Akamai, CacheFlow up +400% at IPO.

ICGE example: $200.94 per share, 287.7 million shares = $57 billion assets worth less than 10% of that.

JDSU worth over $200 billion in 2000 and losing money?

Supply and Demand Drive Stock Prices in the Short-run

Current stock price reflects the amount that the marginal investor, given supply and demand considerations, is willing to pay to acquire as little as 100 shares of a company

In short-run this price may or may not have anything to do with the long-term value of the company.

Current price may be influenced by temporary supply and demand imbalance or by the markets over or under reaction to information.--ENMD

The Ten Principles of Finance Relating to Valuation

11.5 Principle 5: When Analyzing Returns, Simple Averages are Never Simple

- Many investment managers and advisors use simple averages to portray their historic performance
- However, simple averages are a misleading way to assess investment returns—compound or geometric averages are far more representative of actual investment performance

Geometric average is calculated as below:

$$\left(\frac{\text{Value at the end of the period}}{\text{Value at the beginning of the period}} \right)^{1/T}$$

Where T is the number of years in the compounding period

Simple Averages of Percentages are Never Simple

The math underlying investment returns and percentages computes investment gains more favorably than comparable losses.

Problem is embedded in calculation of simple averages. If there is a negative percentage return the calculation of a simple average is biased upwards.

Simple average returns can hide very poor performance.

Simple Averages of Percentages are Never Simple

	Beginning	Ending	Annual
Year	Value	Value	Return
1	$10	$20	100%
2	20	4	-80%
			20%
Simple Average Return			10%
Compound Average Return			-36.75%

Martha's Investment Performance
Simple & Compound Average Returns

_____

_____

_____

_____

_____

_____

_____

_____

The Ten Principles of Finance Relating to Valuation

11.6 <u>Principle 6</u>: Transaction Costs, Taxes and Inflation are Your Enemies

- Transaction cost comes in many forms: brokerage commissions when you execute a trade, sales loads, 12b-1 and redemption fees when you purchase or sell a mutual fund and yearly asset management fees paid to a mutual fund, stockbroker or investment adviser
- Transaction costs and the effects of taxes and inflation can greatly reduce the real returns on your investments
- It should be every investor's mission to reduce her transaction costs to the lowest possible level

_____

_____

_____

_____

_____

_____

The Ten Principles of Finance Relating to Valuation

11.6 Transaction Costs, Taxes and Inflation are Your Enemies

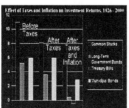

The long-term effect of taxes and inflation on investment returns for common stocks, long-term government bonds, Treasury Bills, and municipal bonds over 1926-1999 is shown in the graph

_____

_____

_____

_____

_____

_____

The Ten Principles of Finance Relating to Valuation

11.6 Transaction Costs, Taxes and Inflation are Your Enemies

- As we observed in the graph, taxes can have a negative effect on investment performance and inflation decreases the real rate of return on the investment
- While inflation is beyond the control of the investor, investor can establish tax-advantaged accounts to accumulate retirement assets and can defer payment of taxes

---

The Ten Principles of Finance Relating to Valuation

11.7 Principle 7: Time and the Value of Money are Closely Related

- A dollar today is worth more than a dollar tomorrow
- To assess if an investment is good, you must be able to compare the value of money that you invest today with the value of the money that you expect to receive in the future and we use the process of compounding and discounting to make the comparison
- Compounding is the process of going from today's value, or present value (PV), to some expected but unknown future value (FV)

The Ten Principles of Finance Relating to Valuation

11.7 Time and the Value of Money are Closely Related

- Future value is the amount of money that an investment will grow to at some future date by earning interest at a certain rate

$$FV = PV * (1 + r)^{\wedge n}$$

- For example if you have a stock worth $10 that increases in value at the rate of 6% per year for five years, the value of stock at the end of five years

$$= \$10 [(1+.06)^{\wedge 5}] = \$13.38$$

The Ten Principles of Finance Relating to Valuation

11.7 Time and the Value of Money are Closely Related

- Discounting is the process of going from an expected future value to a present value
- The math underlying discounting and the calculation of present value is the exact flip side to compounding and future value
- Discount Factor = $1/(1 + r)^n$
- PV = FV * Discount Factor
- For example if you will be receiving $100 in 3 years and the discount rate is 10%, PV= $100 * [$1/(1+.10)^3$] = $75.13

The Ten Principles of Finance Relating to Valuation

11.8 Principle 8: Asset Allocation is a Very Important Decision

- To achieve the highest level of return for the amount of risk we can absorb, we should diversify our investment holdings over an array of assets classes
- The diversification process begins with asset allocation which is dividing investment funds among different asset classes
- The most basic asset classes are cash and short maturity deposits or securities, fixed income securities and bonds, and common stock

The Ten Principles of Finance Relating to Valuation

11.8 Asset Allocation is a Very Important Decision

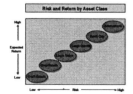

Risk and Return by Asset Class

The trade-off of risk and return that we discussed in Principle 1 also applies to asset classes, and is illustrated in the chart

The Ten Principles of Finance Relating to Valuation

11.8 Asset Allocation is a Very Important Decision

- Asset allocation is generally a personal decision which reflects beliefs about the anticipated risk and return of asset classes

- If you believe the stock market is going to crash, you should lower your stock allocation, shifting moneys to bonds or cash and alternatively if you believe that long-term interest rates are going to rise substantially, you should shift money from bonds into cash

- An element of market timing may be involved in asset allocation

---

The Ten Principles of Finance Relating to Valuation

11.8 Asset Allocation is a Very Important Decision

- Brinson study of investment performance of mutual funds and pension funds research showed that more than 90% of the variability in fund performance over time was attributable to asset allocation-meaning asset allocation is more important than the specific securities that are selected for investment

- Optimal asset allocation for an investor depends upon the risk/return profile of an investor—how much risk can he stomach when it comes to volatility and potential losses in his stock allocation and also depends upon where he is in his financial life cycle

---

The Ten Principles of Finance Relating to Valuation

11.9 Principle 9: Asset Diversification Will Reduce Risk

- To reduce the risk of your portfolio it is important to diversify your holdings
- Diversification means to spread your wealth among a number of different investments
- The goal of diversification is to invest in a group of assets that provides you with the best return possible given a level of risk

The Ten Principles of Finance Relating to Valuation

11.9 Asset Diversification Will Reduce Risk

- When making decisions affecting risk and return, consider the total amount of your assets—your career, house and all of your tangible and financial assets as being held in one portfolio, one pool

- For a first shot at diversification, try to separate your career assets from your investment assets

- Also since the goal of diversification is to reduce the downside risk of your asset base, avoid such things as investing in the stock of the company for which you   work or investing in related industries

---

The Ten Principles of Finance Relating to Valuation

11.9 Asset Diversification Will Reduce Risk

- For financial assets it is important to know that the key to diversification and risk reduction is in the correlation of the   returns of your assets

- Correlation is a statistic used in investing that measures the   degree to which the movements of variables are related

- Correlation is measured on a scale of −1.0 to +1.0

- A correlation coefficient of 0.0 indicates no meaningful relationship between the two assets

---

The Ten Principles of Finance Relating to Valuation

11.9 Asset Diversification Will Reduce Risk

- A correlation coefficient of +1.0 between two stocks mean that when one stock is up 10%, the other stock   will also go up 10% and correlation of −1.0 means that   when one stock is up 5%, the other stock is down 5%

- Assets that are highly correlated offer less risk reduction from diversification than assets that are less correlated

- Diversification reduces the unsystematic risk of a portfolio. Unsystematic risk is specific to a company and Systematic risk represents the risk of the stock market

    Total Risk = Systematic Risk + Unsystematic Risk

The Ten Principles of Finance Relating to Valuation

11.9 Asset Diversification Will Reduce Risk

- Achieving the highest return for each level of risk is known as investing efficiently—investing on the efficient frontier
- Meir Statman study of randomly grouped portfolios of stocks of various sizes to determine the marginal amount of diversification achieved by adding additional stocks to a portfolio showed that just holding 10 stocks reduces volatility to an average of 23.93%, i.e. 50% less than average standard deviation of 49.24% for an individual stock.
- Therefore, diversification greatly reduces risk with no cost.

The Ten Principles of Finance Relating to Valuation

11.9 Asset Diversification Will Reduce Risk

The table below shows how many stocks your portfolio needs to hold to diversify risk

Number of Stocks in Portfolio	Average Std. Dev. of Annual Portfolio Returns	Ratio of Portfolio Std. Dev. of a Single Stock
1	49.24%	100%
10	23.93%	49%
50	20.20%	41%
100	19.69%	40%
300	19.34%	39%
500	19.27%	39%
1000	19.21%	39%

The Ten Principles of Finance Relating to Valuation

11.9 Asset Diversification Will Reduce Risk

- Diversification, while limiting your risk by spreading them over a larger number of securities, also limits the gains you would have received if you had concentrated your investments in a few stocks that turned out to be incredible winners
- To diversify intelligently apart from carefully investing career-oriented assets, house, and investments in your employer, divide the amount that you have allocated to your stock portfolio into twenty-5% increments and invest those increments in a combination of stocks and no-load mutual funds

The Ten Principles of Finance Relating to Valuation

11.9 Asset Diversification Will Reduce Risk

- If you are extremely bullish on a particular stock that you own, allow your relative portfolio percentage to increase, either through the appreciation in price of the stock over time or through an additional purchase, to a maximum 10% of your equity portfolio

- Any portion over 10% should be sold when you rebalance your equity portfolio, which should be performed on an annual basis

- You could also combine the proportions of individual stocks and mutual funds to achieve your desired stock asset class allocation

---

The Ten Principles of Finance Relating to Valuation

11.10 Principle 10: An Asset Pricing Model Should be Used to Value Investments

- The Capital Asset Pricing Model (CAPM) is a simple model that estimates the rate of return an investor should expect to receive on a risky asset

- In valuation, its principal purpose is to determine the discount rate to use when valuing an asset

- CAPM states that the expected return of a risky asset, $E(R_i)$, such as a common stock, is equal to the return on the risk-free asset (R_f) plus a risk premium

---

The Ten Principles of Finance Relating to Valuation

11.10 An Asset Pricing Model Should be Used to Value Investments

Expected Return = Risk-Free Rate + Risk Premium

$$E(R_i) = R_f + \beta_i * [E(R_m) - R_f]$$

- The risk-free rate (R_f) that we use for valuation is the rate on the long-term (10-year) Treasury bond

- The risk premium is a function of two factors: the stock's beta (β_i), and the market risk premium, which is the expected return on the overall stock market (R_m) minus the risk free rate: $[E(R_m) - R_f]$

The Ten Principles of Finance Relating to Valuation

11.10 Principle 10: An Asset Pricing Model Should be Used to Value Investments

- The Capital Asset Pricing Model (CAPM) is a simple model that estimates the rate of return an investor should expect to receive on a risky asset
- In valuation, its principal purpose is to determine the discount rate to use when valuing an asset
- CAPM states that the expected return of a risky asset, $E(R_i)$, such as a common stock, is equal to the return on the risk-free asset (R_f) plus a risk premium

---

The Ten Principles of Finance Relating to Valuation

11.10 Principle 10: An Asset Pricing Model Should be Used to Value Investments

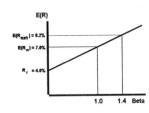

If the stock market prices stocks in the manner consistent with the Capital Asset Pricing Model, the expected return on each stock should fall on the diagonal risk/return line shown in the chart

---

The Ten Principles of Finance Relating to Valuation

11.10 An Asset Pricing Model Should be Used to Value Investments

CAPM Example: Suppose the risk free rate is 4% and an expected return on the stock market is 6% and if beta of XYZ Inc is 1.2 calculate the expected return of XYZ Inc.

$$E(R_{xyz}) = R_f + \beta_i * [E(R_m) - R_f]$$
$$E(R_{xyz}) = 4\% + 1.2\ (6\% - 4\%)$$
$$= 6.4\%$$

CAPM is a very simple yet powerful way to estimate the cost of equity, which is usually the most significant component of a company's weighted cost of capital

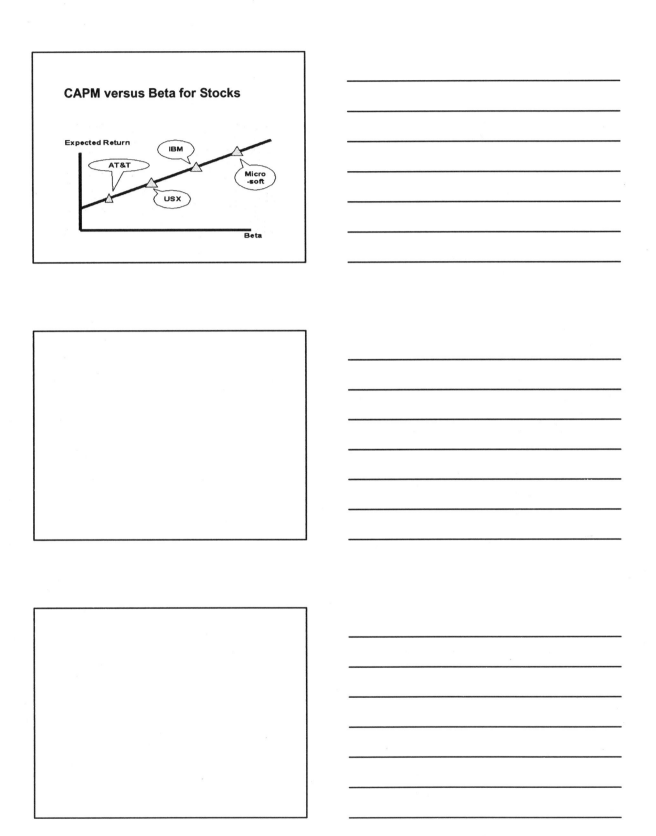

Risk and Return and the Capital Asset Pricing Model

Chapter 12: Risk and Return and the Capital Asset Pricing Model

Woolridge & Gray

An Important Principle of Finance: CAPM-The Trade-Off Between Return and Risk

In the investment world there is a trade-off between the expected return on an investment and its risk.

An investment such as a short-term Treasury Bill (no default risk and little price volatility) has a lower expected return (e.g. 4%) than a stock (large price volatility) with higher expected returns (e.g. 10%).

We measure risk by an investment's price or return volatility—over what range can the price/return of an investment move. More price/return movement—greater risk. The price of a stock can go from $225 to $0.50—Internet Capital Group.

A rational investor requires a higher expected return to accept additional risk. The model that describes the trade-off between expected return and risk is the Capital Asset Pricing Model (CAPM).

Risk and Return and the Capital Asset Pricing Model

Risk Return Relationship

There is a direct tradeoff between the expected rate of return on an asset and its risk. The tradeoff is represented by the diagonal line in the diagram below

Risk and Return and the Capital Asset Pricing Model

12.3 Historic Returns by Asset Class

Does lower risk investments generally have offered lower returns and higher risk investments have offered higher returns? The results of the Ibbotson and Sinquefield study is shown below:

	Return	Std Deviation
Treasury Bills	3.8%	3.2%
Government Bonds	5.3%	9.4%
Corporate Bonds	5.8%	8.6%
Large Company Stock	10.7%	20.2%
Small Company Stock	12.5%	33.2%

Long-Term Return and Risk of U.S. Securities

1926-1999

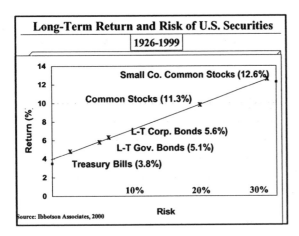

Small Co. Common Stocks (12.6%)

Common Stocks (11.3%)

L-T Corp. Bonds 5.6%)

L-T Gov. Bonds (5.1%)

Treasury Bills (3.8%)

Return (%)

Risk

Source: Ibbotson Associates, 2000

What do we mean by Rate of Return?

Rate of Return = (Cash Payment + Change in Price)/Price Paid;

You Buy IBM @ $90, receive a cash dividend of $4, and sell it one year later at $104;

Rate of Return = ($4 + $14) / ($90) = .2 = 20%

Components of Rate of Return

Cash Payments-**Dividends** and **Interest** are taxed as ordinary income (i.e. up to 39%):

Dividends- quarterly payments made on some stocks (ownership)

Interest- semi-annual payments made on bonds (debt)

Change in Price- **Capital Gain** or **Capital Loss**

Can be realized- you sell your asset and incur gain or loss, or unrealized- you continue to own your asset

If realized, the gains or losses are taxed

Long-term gains and losses (asset owned for longer than one year) are taxed at a lower rate (e.g. 20%)

Short-term gains and losses (asset owned for less than one year) are taxed at a higher rate (e.g. up to 39%)

What do we mean by Risk?

Risk is measured by the possible range of returns around an expected return;

Usually measured by a statistic called the **standard deviation of returns**;

Risk has both **negative** and **positive** outcomes. It generates returns that are **lower** than expected or **higher** than expected.

Risk and Return and the Capital Asset Pricing Model

12.2 Definitions Relating to Return and Risk

Standard Deviation of Return - (σ):

- Overall risk on an asset is usually measured by the variability of returns
- The standard deviation is the statistic that is normally used to measure how wildly or tightly the observed stock returns cluster around the average stock return
- A higher standard deviation means more fluctuations and greater risk

Risk and Return and the Capital Asset Pricing Model

12.2 Definitions Relating to Return and Risk

Calculation of Standard Deviation of Return - (σ):

Example

- Suppose the annual returns of stock of XYZ Inc. for the last three years was

Year 1 – 8%

Year 2 – (1%)

Year 3 – 2%

Risk and Return and the Capital Asset Pricing Model

12.2 Definitions Relating to Return and Risk
Calculation of Standard Deviation of Return - (σ):

Step 1 - Take the simple average return of the distribution of returns

Year	Return	Average Return		
1	8%	3%		
2	(1%)	3%		
3	2%	3%		
Total	9%			

Risk and Return and the Capital Asset Pricing Model

12.2 Definitions Relating to Return and Risk
Calculation of Standard Deviation of Return - (σ):

Step 2 - Take each individual observed return and subtract the average of the returns

Year	Return	Average Return	Deviation of Return	
1	8%	3%	5%	
2	(1%)	3%	(4%)	
3	2%	3%	(1%)	
Total	9%			

189

Risk and Return and the Capital Asset Pricing Model

12.2 Definitions Relating to Return and Risk Calculation of Standard Deviation of Return - (σ):

Step 3 - Square the resulting difference and add the squares to get the sum of the squares

Year	Return	Average Return	Deviation of Return	Squared Deviation
1	8%	3%	5%	0.0025
2	(1%)	3%	(4%)	0.0016
3	2%	3%	(1%)	0.0001
Total	9%			0.0042

Risk and Return and the Capital Asset Pricing Model

12.2 Definitions Relating to Return and Risk Calculation of Standard Deviation of Return - (σ):

Step 4 - Divide the sum of the squares by the total number of observations minus 1—the result is the variance of the distribution

Variance = 0.0042/(3-1) = 0.0021

Step 5 - Take the square root of the variance to get the standard deviation of the returns

Standard Deviation = 0.0021 ^ 1/2 = 4.58%

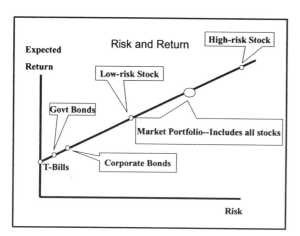

Capital Asset Pricing Model (CAPM)

From the Risk-Return Line, we can estimate the expected return on a stock, $E(R_i)$;

Expected return on stock (i), $E(R_i)$ equals the Risk-Free Rate (R_f) + the stock's Beta (β_i) times the Market Risk Premium—the return on the market (R_m) minus (R_f).

$$E(R_i) = R_f + \beta_i * (R_m - R_f)$$

---

20 th Century Averages for American Investments

		Risk Premium
Treasury Bills	4%	----
Government Bonds	5%	1%
Corporate Bonds	6%	2%
Average Common Stock	12%	8%

Our Questions For Today

How do we measure risk of an asset?

Answer: Beta

What's the relation between beta and return?

Answer: It's very positive

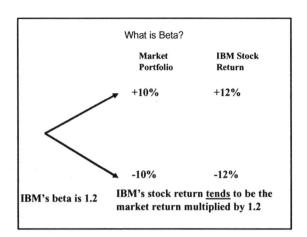

What is Beta?

	Market Portfolio	IBM Stock Return
	+10%	+12%
	-10%	-12%

IBM's beta is 1.2   **IBM's stock return <u>tends</u> to be the market return multiplied by 1.2**

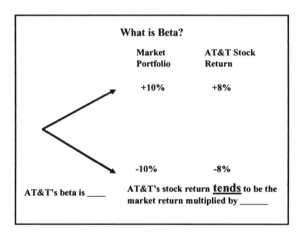

What is Beta?

	Market Portfolio	AT&T Stock Return
	+10%	+8%
	-10%	-8%

AT&T's beta is _____   **AT&T's stock return <u>tends</u> to be the market return multiplied by _____**

A Quick Quiz on Beta

Firm	Market up 20%	Market down 20%	Firm's Beta
Intel	30%	-30%	1.50
GE	15%	-15%	0.75
Apple	20%	-20%	1.00

Why is beta a measure of "Market Magnification"?

A stock with a beta of 2 will tend to double market movements (up or down)

A stock with a beta of 0.50 will tend to have movements (up or down) equal to ½ the market

---

Isn't there more to Risk than Beta?

Yes. There is <u>unsystematic</u> or <u>firm specific risk</u>—a risk that affects the return of that firm or industry only—such as a labor strike or an accounting scandal on the <u>downside</u>, or a new discovery or breakthrough product on the <u>upside</u>.

<u>On average, the firm specific risks average out to be zero</u>, if an investor diversifies her portfolio and holds a large number of stocks (over 20 stocks in unrelated industries).

Finance theory assumes that investors are rational and own diversified portfolios, so the risk that we focus on is <u>systematic</u> or <u>market-related risk</u> as measured by <u>Beta</u>.

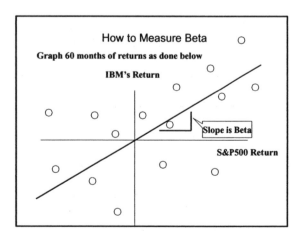

How to Measure Beta

Graph 60 months of returns as done below

IBM's Return

Slope is Beta

S&P500 Return

Using Beta to determine Expected Returns

What is a risk premium?

The amount by which an investment is expected to outperform T-Bills or the average amount by which an investment has outperformed T-Bills in the past

The Market has averaged 12% a year

T-Bills have averaged 4% a year

The market risk premium is __8%__?

An investment's beta determines its risk premium

T-Bill Rate: 4%

Expected return on Market: 8%

Market risk-premium= 4%

AOL has a beta of 1.6

AOL's risk-premium = 1.6 * 4% = 6.4%

AOL's expected return = 4% + 6.4% = 10.4%

An investment's beta determines its risk premium

T-Bill Rate: 4%

Expected return on Market: 8%

Market risk-premium= 4%

ATT has a beta of 0.6

ATT's risk-premium = 0.6 * 4% = 2.4%

ATT's expected return = 4% + 2.4% = 6.4%

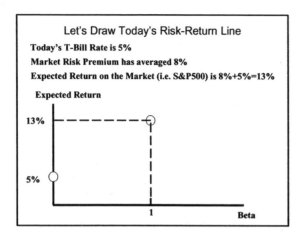

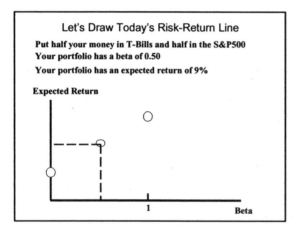

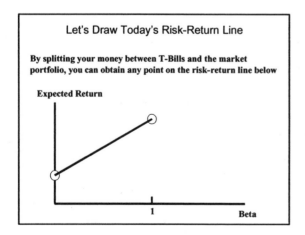

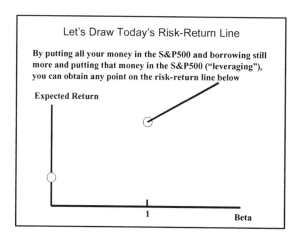

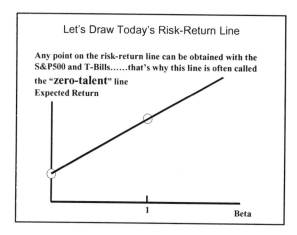

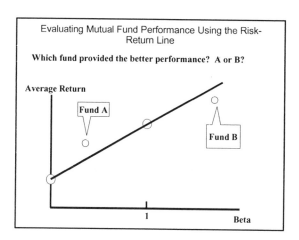

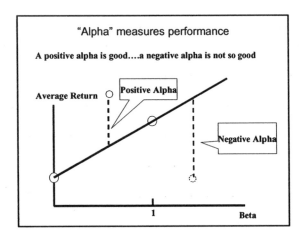

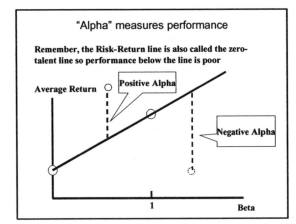

A Practice Problem

T-Bills averaged 4% over last few years

S&P 500 averaged 14%

The XYZ Fund had an average return of 16% and a beta of 1.4

Find XYZ's alpha

The CAPM risk-return line for a beta of 1.4 is at   4% + [1.4 * 10%] = 18%

XYZ's alpha is 16%-18% = -2%

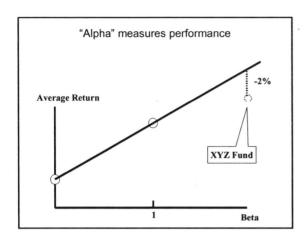

A Practice Problem

T-Bills averaged 4% over last few years

S&P500 averaged 14%

The Nittany Lion Fund had an average return of 16% and a beta of 0.80

Find Nittany Lion's alpha

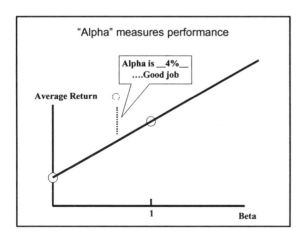

Efficient Capital Markets and Random Walks

Chapter 13: Efficient Capital Markets and Random Walks

Woolridge & Gray

Review of Some Definitions

$\underline{\text{CAPM}} = E(R_i) = R_f + \beta_i * (R_m - R_f)$

$\underline{\text{Market Risk Premium}} = (R_m - R_f)$

$\underline{\text{Beta}} = \text{Risk} = \beta_i = [E(R_i) - R_f] / (R_m - R_f)$

$\underline{\text{Alpha}}$ = Observed Return of Asset – Expected Return of Asset

$\underline{\text{Unsystematic Risk}}$ or firm specific risk- the risk that can be diversified away

$\underline{\text{Systematic Risk}}$- market related risk as measured by Beta. Can not be diversified away

---

A Practice Problem

T-Bills averaged 5% over last few years

S&P 500 averaged 15%

The ABC Fund had an average return of 14% and a beta of 0.80

According to the CAPM, <u>what is the fund's expected return</u> on the risk-return line?

CAPM Equation: $E(R_i) = R_f + \beta_i * (R_m - R_f)$

Expected Return = 5% + .8(15% - 5%) = 13%

<u>Find ABC's alpha</u>

Alpha = Observed Return – Expected Return

Alpha = 14% - 13% = 1%

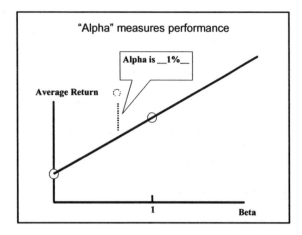

"Alpha" measures performance

Alpha is __1%__

Alpha Applied to Mutual Funds

Gross Return means "<u>before expenses</u>"
<u>Net Return</u> = Gross Return - Expenses

For XYZ, gross return = 11.4%

For XYZ, expense ratio is 1.2%
(about average for stock funds)

What is XYZ's net return?

Net Return = 11.4% - 1.2% = 10.2%

Mutual Fund Performance
Use this information for your own investing

Using <u>gross returns</u>, the <u>average fund</u> has an alpha of 0%

What is the average alpha using <u>net returns</u>?

-1.2%

Is good performance in the <u>past</u> (using gross returns) an indicator of good future performance?

<u>NO</u>!!

89% of funds failed to match the S&P500 over the past 5 years

Index Funds are hard to beat

A good practice question

The XYZ fund had a positive alpha using gross returns over the past five years. What is its expected alpha using gross returns for the next five years?

Answer: 0%

Using net returns?

Negative the amount of expenses

An Important Principle of Finance: Efficient Capital Markets

Asset prices react very quickly to the receipt of new information.

New information is random and can either be good—and drive stock prices higher, or bad—and propel stock prices lower.

The quick reaction of many market participants to the new information tends to drive prices to their "correct" level.

What is an "EFFICIENT MARKET"?

A market where all investments are accurately priced

This means there are no good investments

Also, there are no bad investments

Each investment offers an expected return to match its level of risk

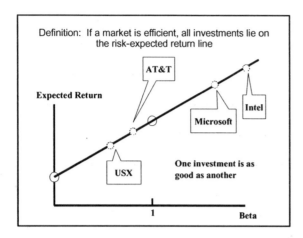

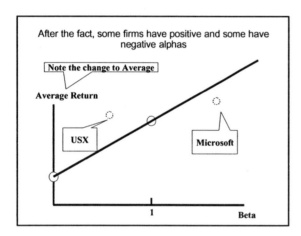

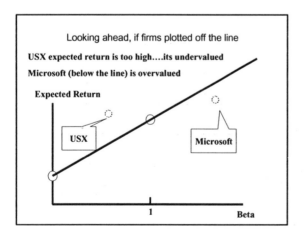

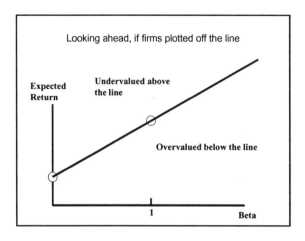

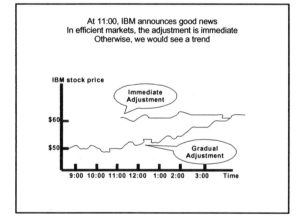

Efficient Capital Markets and Random Walks

Random Walk Hypothesis:

- A random walk is a path that a variable takes, such as the observed price of a stock, where the future direction of the path (up or down) can't be predicted solely on the basis of past movements

- Share prices react immediately to news so that there is no predictable trend implied by a more gradual share price adjustment. Also, the next news event leading to the next immediate adjustment cannot be predicted. Therefore, in an efficient market, share price changes are random

Efficient Capital Markets and Random Walks

13.2 Types of Market Efficiency

Weak form efficiency:

Weak form efficiency implies that stock prices reflect the information contained in the history of past stock prices and trading volume. This notion implies that daily stock price changes are independent and thus it is useless for investors to try to detect and exploit trends in stock prices. This is the random walk hypothesis according to which stock prices are random and unpredictable.

Efficient Capital Markets and Random Walks

13.2 Types of Market Efficiency

Semi-strong form efficiency:

Semi-strong form efficiency indicates that stock prices should reflect all publicly available information. According to this proposition, stock prices react very, very quickly to new economic, industrial, and company disclosures thereby prohibiting investors from earning abnormal returns.

Efficient Capital Markets and Random Walks

13.2 Types of Market Efficiency

Strong-form efficiency :

According to strong-form efficiency, stock prices reflect all information, including information not available to the investment community.

Efficient Capital Markets and Random Walks

13.3 Tests of Market Efficiency

- The goal of many of the studies has been to find an investment strategy that consistently produces investment returns, adjusted for risk, that are greater than the returns associated with a long-term buy-and- hold strategy for a diversified portfolio of stocks
- The majority of studies have shown that new information is quickly incorporated into stock prices and the excess returns that are associated with certain stock selection strategies are arbitraged away and that stock market is relatively efficient, or at least semi-efficient

Efficient Capital Markets and Random Walks

13.3 Tests of Market Efficiency

Behavioral Finance:

- Academicians who specialize in the field of behavioral finance, have challenged Modern Portfolio Theory's assumption that investors are rational and markets behave rationally.
- Behavioral theorists have conducted studies that show that stock markets were not efficient and people and markets, at times, behave irrationally.

Efficient Capital Markets and Random Walks

13.3 Tests of Market Efficiency

The Fama and French Study:

- Fama and French study compares the performance of the returns associated with portfolios of stocks that have certain similar characteristics
- The study showed, among other things, portfolios of stock with a high book value (BE) to market value (ME) ratio consistently outperformed portfolios with low (BE/ME) ratios and called to question the validity of efficient capital markets

Efficient Capital Markets and Random Walks

13.3 Tests of Market Efficiency

The Fama and French Study (Contd.):

▪ The study also found that stocks with high earnings to price ratios consistently outperformed portfolios of stocks with low earnings to price ratios and that stocks with small market capitalization outperformed stocks with large market capitalization.

▪ Other researchers have conducted studies based upon the F&F study with roughly the same results.

Efficient Capital Markets and Random Walks

13.3 Tests of Market Efficiency

Less Technical Evidence from the Real World:

▪ Much evidence indicates that stock price changes are independent

▪ Most evidence indicates stock prices react immediately to news announcements and excess returns are arbitraged away

---

Efficient Capital Markets and Random Walks

13.3 Tests of Market Efficiency

Evidence From Mutual Funds:

▪ Studying performance of Mutual Funds over time using gross returns and calculating alpha has shown that on average, mutual funds do no better than to lie on the risk-return line i.e. an alpha of zero.

▪ Therefore net returns i.e. gross returns less fees, will give a negative alpha.

▪ Thus in an efficient market, a mutual fund customer can on average earn the highest alpha by choosing the funds with the lowest fees.

Efficient Capital Markets and Random Walks

13.3 Tests of Market Efficiency

Evidence on Individual Investors:

- Professors Brad Barber and Terrance Odean's study of investment performance for 60,000 individual and household accounts at a major discount brokerage firm showed that trading costs negatively and significantly affect the returns of market participants.
- Thus an individual investor can improve returns by reducing transactions costs to the lowest level possible.

Bond Valuation and Interest Rates

Chapter 14: Bond Valuation and Interest Rates

Woolridge & Gray

Bond Valuation and Interest Rates

Chapter Objectives

- Bonds - their structure and risks
- How bonds are issued in the primary market and traded in the secondary markets
- How to value a bond
- Interest rates and how interest rates affect bond valuation

---

Bond Valuation and Interest Rates

Chapter Overview

- 14.1   Bonds in General
- 14.2   Bonds and Risk
- 14.3   Types of Bonds and Trading Activity
- 14.4   Interest Rates, Default Risk, Other Factors and Bond Yields
- 14.5   Valuing a Bond

Bond Valuation and Interest Rates

14.1 Bonds in General

- A bond is a debt financial contract under which the issuer is obligated to make periodic interest payments and repay the principal at some pre-determined time
- The legal agreement between the issuer of the bonds and the investors is known as indenture
- The amount that is originally borrowed and the amount that is repaid when the bonds mature and the principal payment is due is known as principal value, or par amount or a maturity value

---

Bond Valuation and Interest Rates

Structure of Interest Payments on Bonds:

- The interest rate on a bond is the annual interest, expressed on a percentage basis, which accrues or is paid by the issuer to the owner of the bond
- Interest rate setting structures vary and can be broadly classified into two categories
  - Fixed Rate Structures
  - Floating Rate Structures
- Interest rate setting structures affect the value of a bond

---

Bond Valuation and Interest Rates

Fixed Rate Structures:

- The interest rates and payments are fixed over the life of the bond, and the investors and the issuer are certain of the payments
- In a Fixed Rate Par Bond, the issuer issues the bond at par value and pays fixed interest semi annually on predetermined dates and repays the full par value of the bond on maturity

Bond Valuation and Interest Rates

Fixed Rate Structures:

- In a <u>Fixed Rate Discount Bond</u>, the bond is issued at an interest rate that creates a market value of less than par at the time of pricing, and offering an yield that is higher than the coupon rate
- In a <u>Fixed Rate Premium Bond</u>, the issuer will market a bond with a coupon and interest rate that creates a market value of more than par at the time of pricing, and an offering yield that is lower than the coupon rate

Bond Valuation and Interest Rates

Floating Rate Structures:

- In <u>floating interest rate</u> instruments, initially interest rate setting mechanisms were based upon some interest rate index or level of a risk free security
- Over the years, rate setting mechanisms have been developed that are designed to create a bond that always trades at or near par value
- Historically, the floating interest rates have been significantly lower than the rates on fixed-coupon bonds. However, the issuer retains the <u>interest rate risk</u> inherent in a bond issue

Bond Valuation and Interest Rates

Security:

- The sources of security on a bond issue can vary a great deal, and will affect the credit rating and creditworthiness of the issue
- Securities that are issued by the U.S. Government are usually assumed to be risk-free
- Municipal bonds may be secured in a variety of ways such as by the issuer's taxing power, revenues and credit enhancement devices

Bond Valuation and Interest Rates

Security:

- Corporate debt is most often an unsecured promise by the corporation to pay its debts. Sometimes the bonds will be secured by collateral or a mortgage on a particular property or piece of equipment
- Asset-backed securities are secured by the sponsor who structures the financing and usually purchases credit enhancement

---

Bond Valuation and Interest Rates

Optional Redemption:

- <u>Call Option</u>: Issuer's option to redeem bonds prior to their stated maturity, at a pre-determined price above par value
- <u>Call Premium</u>: The excess amount of the call price above the par value
- An investor that owns a <u>callable bond</u> is subject to considerable uncertainty about cash flows on its callable bonds and hence will require a higher yield on callable bonds than on comparable non-callable bonds

---

Bond Valuation and Interest Rates

14.2 Bonds and Risk

<u>Four types of risk</u> involved while investing in fixed-rate or fixed-coupon debt obligations are:

- <u>Default risk</u> - the risk that the bond will not pay interest or principal when due
- <u>Reinvestment risk</u> - the unknown rate at which cash inflows may be reinvested
- <u>Prepayment risk</u> - when an issuer calls a bond prior to its maturity
- <u>Interest rate risk</u> - the risk that a change in market interest rates will affect the value of the bond

Bond Valuation and Interest Rates

Default Risk and Bond Ratings:

- All taxable fixed-rate debt that is issued or traded in the U.S. capital markets is priced at what is called a spread to Treasuries which is the measure of default risk on an asset-backed transaction or a specific company's debt
- The interest rate, or yield, of all debt is vitally dependent on the risk-free rate associated with the comparable maturity U.S. Treasury debt
- This spread will change over time depending on economic conditions and the relative default risk associated with the specific debt security

Bond Valuation and Interest Rates

Spread to Treasuries

- The difference between the yield on a non-callable U.S. Treasury bond and the yield on a non-callable corporate bond with an identical maturity is called the spread to Treasuries and is a measure of the default premium associated with the corporate bond
- The spread to Treasuries is a function of the type of industry the issuer belongs, the credit rating of the corporate bond and a function of the time to maturity of the bond

Bonds Online Corporate Yield Curve-www.bonds-online.com/ (8/29/03)

Reuters Corporate Spreads for Banks

Spreads compiled using [Reuters Evaluators ▼] [Refresh] [Download spread]

Rating	1 yr	2 yr	3 yr	5 yr	7 yr	10 yr	30 yr
Aaa/AAA	21	28	35	42	57	69	89
Aa1/AA+	30	39	40	51	67	80	100
Aa2/AA	32	43	47	55	70	82	103
Aa3/AA-	34	48	49	60	74	86	112
A1/A+	58	64	68	73	90	104	127
A2/A	61	67	70	77	92	106	131
A3/A-	63	70	73	81	95	109	132
Baa1/BBB+	78	89	97	106	138	160	186
Baa2/BBB	81	97	105	113	143	166	191
Baa3/BBB-	88	102	110	117	148	173	196
Ba1/BB+	325	335	543	555	775	593	615
Ba2/BB	535	545	555	565	585	605	625
Ba3/BB-	545	555	565	575	595	615	635
B1/B+	690	700	710	740	780	820	870
B2/B	700	710	720	750	790	830	880
B3/B-	710	720	730	760	800	840	890
Caa/CCC	1110	1120	1130	1155	1165	1175	1205

Bond Valuation and Interest Rates

Default Risk and Bond Ratings:

- Three rating agencies - Moody's Investors Services, Standard & Poor's Corporation, and Fitch Ratings Ltd. specialize in rating the default risk and credit worthiness of a bond issue and of corporate, municipal, and even sovereign government issuers
- The agencies then assign the issue with a bond rating that ranges from the equivalent of AAA, the highest grade with a very remote chance of default, down to CCC, the lowest grade and currently in default
- The ratings have significant bearing on the required yield on a bond in the marketplace

---

Bond Ratings

TABLE 1   Bond Ratings by Moody's and Standard and Poor's

Rating			
Moody's	Standard and Poor's	Description	Examples of Corporations with Bonds Outstanding in 2002
Aaa	AAA	Highest quality (lowest default risk)	General Electric, Pfizer Inc., Road Management Services Inc
Aa	AA	High quality	Hewlett-Packard, Mobil Oil, Upjohn Inc., Wal-Mart
A	A	Upper medium grade	Anheuser-Busch, McDonalds Inc., Motorola Inc.
Baa	BBB	Medium grade	Albertson's, Ford Motor, Marriott
Ba	BB	Lower medium grade	Rite-Aid Corp., Rayo Vac, Six Flags Theme Park
B	B	Speculative	Revlon, Mary Kay Inc., U.S. Can Inc
Caa	CCC, CC	Poor (high default risk)	U.S. Airways Inc.,
Ca	C	Highly speculative	Metrocall,
C	D	Lowest grade	KMart, Carmike Cinemas, Enron

Bond Valuation and Interest Rates

Default Risk and Bond Ratings:

- Beyond the corporate credit risk rating is the risk classification specific to a particular bond issue of the company
- Senior debt is usually the most secure debt issued by a company. In the event of liquidation in bankruptcy, the most senior debt is paid first and whatever is leftover is distributed to the rest of the debt holders
- Subordinated debt is debt that follows senior debt in line for claims on cash flows and assets upon liquidation

Bond Valuation and Interest Rates

Reinvestment Risk:

- <u>Reinvestment risk</u> is the risk that arises from reinvesting the periodic interest payments on fixed-rate bonds
- An investor receiving payments over the life of a coupon-bearing bond faces the risk of reinvesting coupon payments at uncertain future interest rates than may be lower than the yield on the bond
- The yield to maturity on coupon bonds depends significantly on the reinvestment rates

Bond Valuation and Interest Rates

Prepayment Risk:

- <u>Prepayment risk</u> is the risk that a bond will be retired or redeemed at a time earlier than its maturity date
- The call options and redemption features in debt instruments introduce uncertainty into the expected cash flows. This uncertainty has a cost, in the way of a higher rate of interest on the bonds

Bond Valuation and Interest Rates

Interest Rate Risk:

- <u>Interest rate risk</u> is often the most difficult risk to assess
- The price volatility of a bond is the extent to which its price changes with fluctuations in market levels of interest rates
- Bond prices and yields move in opposite directions, other things being equal. The magnitude of price movements will differ based on specific bond characteristics

Bond Valuation and Interest Rates

Interest Rate Risk:

The longer the maturity of a bond, the higher the volatility of bond prices

The table below gives the price change for a 1% increase in yield:

Maturity	Coupon	Yield	Price	% Change
10	6%	7%	$92.89	-7.11%
20	6%	7%	$89.32	-10.68%
30	6%	7%	$87.53	-12.47%

Bond Valuation and Interest Rates

Interest Rate Risk:

The lower the coupon on a bond, the higher the price volatility

The table below gives the price change for a 1% increase in yield:

Coupon	Yield	Price	Yield	Price	% Change
0%	6%	$16.97	7%	$12.69	-25.23%
6%	6%	$100.00	7%	$87.53	-12.47%
12%	6%	$183.02	7%	$162.36	-11.29%

Bond Valuation and Interest Rates

Duration:

- The price volatility of a debt issue is measured using duration
- The duration of a bond is measured in units of time (for example, 7.3 years).
- In the simplest case, the duration of a zero coupon bond is equal to its current time to maturity
- The higher the current coupon payments, the lower the price volatility and the shorter the duration

Bond Valuation and Interest Rates

Duration:

Duration is also defined as a percentage change in the price of an asset, divided by a change in interest rates, and can be represented by the following equation:

$$D = \frac{- P/P}{y}$$

Where: D = Duration, P = dollar price of a bond, P = change in dollar price of a bond, y = market yield, and y = change in market yield

- There is an inverse relationship between interest rate movements and bond prices

Bond Valuation and Interest Rates

Yield Curve:

- The yield curve is the relationship between the yields and the maturities on Treasury securities.
- The yield curve usually is positively sloped which means that investors require higher returns for longer maturity Treasury securities. This is because the prices of longer maturity bonds are more volatile and therefore are viewed as being riskier than shorter maturity securities

Bond Valuation and Interest Rates

14.3 Types of Bonds and Trading Activity

Treasury Securities and the Treasury Market:

- The market for U.S. Treasury securities is the largest and most liquid of any financial markets
- Treasury notes have maturities of one-to-seven years, and bonds have maturities of over seven years
- These securities pay interest on a semi-annual basis over the life the issue, and then the investor gets the principle back at maturity
- Treasury securities' prices fluctuate daily in response to changes in interest rates and the economy

---

Bloomberg Treasury Yield
Curve (8/29/03)

Notes/Bonds

	COUPON	MATURITY DATE	CURRENT PRICE/YIELD	PRICE/YIELD CHANGE	T3?
2-Year	2.000	08/31/2005	100-02/1.96	-0-02/0.032	2
3-Year	2.375	08/15/2006	99-22/2.49	-0-03/0.033	2
5-Year	3.250	08/15/2008	99-02/3.45	-0-07/0.052	2
10-Year	4.250	08/15/2013	98-11/4.46	-0-11/0.044	2
30-Year	5.375	02/15/2031	102-07/5.22	-0-07/0.015	2

CURRENT   PREVIOUS

Bond Valuation and Interest Rates

Municipal Bonds and the Municipal Market:

- <u>Municipal bonds</u> are debt instruments issued by states, cities, municipal authorities and other entities
- Municipal bond interest income is <u>exempt from federal and certain state and local income taxation</u>
- Investor can compare Municipal Bonds interest income with after-tax income of other fixed-income securities, taking into account the investor's marginal tax bracket
- The municipal bond market is a huge, diverse, and extremely complicated marketplace

Bond Valuation and Interest Rates

Municipal Bonds Example:

An investor in the 30% tax bracket purchases a municipal bond that pays a tax-exempt interest rate of 6%. Calculate the taxable equivalent municipal bond yield

Taxable Equivalent Bond Yield $= \dfrac{r}{1-t} = \dfrac{6.00}{(1-0.3)} = 8.6\%$

Bond Valuation and Interest Rates

Taxable Bonds and the Taxable Bond Market:

- Corporations issue bonds to finance their long-term capital needs and to take advantage of tax deduction associated with the interest payments on debt
- Bonds are issued in the primary market at a yield based on the spread to Treasuries that is required for an issue with the appropriate risk
- Corporations also issue bonds known as <u>convertible bonds</u> that usually pays a fixed-rate of interest, and after a certain period of time, can be converted into a fixed number of shares of the issuing corporation

Bond Valuation and Interest Rates

Taxable Bonds and the Taxable Bond Market:

- <u>Mortgage-backed bonds</u> and the <u>asset-backed bonds</u>, secured by car loans, credit card receivables, and other structured bond issues are usually created by financial institutions that originate the loans that are then pooled and marketed to institutional investors
- These bonds are sold to investors in the primary market through an investment banking syndicate and are traded in the secondary over-the counter market

Bond Valuation and Interest Rates

**14.4 Interest Rates, Default Risk, Other Factors
and Bond Yields**

The yield or return that an investor should expect to
receive on a financial asset such as a bond is a function
of a number of factors, the most important of which are:

- The time value of money
- The default risk associated with a particular security
- The liquidity premium and other bond specific factors
  peculiar to the financial asset, such as call provisions

Bond Valuation and Interest Rates

The Term Structure of Interest Rates:

- The yield curve, also known as the term structure of
  interest rates, describes the relationship between the
  yield on a security and its maturity
- The shape of the yield curve, depending on the rate of
  inflation or deflation, the economy and monetary
  policies, can be upward sloping - which is the most
  common, downward sloping - when a significant
  slowdown in inflation is anticipated, flat, or humped

Bond Valuation and Interest Rates

The Term Structure of Interest Rates:

- Several hypotheses attempt to explain the term
  structure of interest rates and the information that it
  conveys to the market
- The three most common explanations are:
  - Pure expectations hypothesis
  - The liquidity preference hypothesis
  - The market segmentation hypothesis

Bond Valuation and Interest Rates

Pure Expectations Hypothesis:

- Under <u>Pure expectations hypothesis</u> the yield curve can be analyzed as a series of expected future short-term interest rates that will adjust in a way such that investors will receive equivalent holding period returns
- Thus the expected average annual return on a long-term bond is the compound average of the expected short-term interest rates
- Thus an upward-sloping yield curve means that investors expect higher future short-term interest rates and a downward-sloping yield curve implies expectations of lower future short-term rates

Bond Valuation and Interest Rates

The Liquidity Preference Hypothesis :

- According to the <u>liquidity preference theory</u> most investors prefer to hold short-term maturity securities and hence in order to induce investors to hold bonds with longer maturities, the issuer must pay a higher interest rate as a liquidity premium
- Thus under this theory, long-term rates are composed of <u>expected short-term rates plus a liquidity premium which increases with time to maturity</u>
- This theory implies an upward-sloping yield curve even when investors expect that short-term rates will remain constant

Relationship Between the Liquidity Premium and Pure Expectations Theory

220

Bond Valuation and Interest Rates

The Market Segmentation Hypothesis :

- The <u>market segmentation hypothesis</u> or the preferred habitat hypothesis, recognizes that the market is composed of diverse investors who have different preferred habitats i.e. short term and long term investments for the investment requirements
- In order to induce investors to move away from their preferred position on the yield curve, an issuer must pay a premium. Thus any maturities that do not have a balance of supply and demand will sell at a premium or discount to their expected yields and the shape of the yield curve is dependent upon demand and supply

Bond Valuation and Interest Rates

Yield Curve as a Predictor of Short-Term Rates:

- Based on empirical evidence, the yield curve has been a particularly poor predictor of future short-term interest rates
- However the rates implied by the pure expectations model of the yield curve is important because trading activity can effectively lock in the forward and zero-coupon rates that are implied in the yield curve, the yield discount rates can be used to value cash flows associated with bonds and valuation of derivatives

Bond Valuation and Interest Rates

The Yield Curve, Inflation and Deflation:

- <u>Nominal interest rate</u> is the actual rate of return or yield associated with an investment (not adjusting for the effect of inflation or deflation)
- The <u>real rate of interest</u> is defined as the difference between the nominal rate of interest and the rate of inflation

  Example: If inflation is 2% and nominal interest rate of 10 year Treasury bond is 6%, then:

  real rate of interest = 6% - 2% = 4%

Bond Valuation and Interest Rates

Call Features and Other Factors:

- The yield level on a bond is influenced by its liquidity, call features and other factors
- With greater liquidity the bonds are more marketable and there is less of a liquidity yield premium associated with the bond
- Investors analyzing a corporate, municipal, or asset-backed bond assign a premium in the way of a higher interest rate to reflect any optional and extraordinary call provisions in the issue

---

Bond Valuation and Interest Rates

Calculating Bond Yield:

- A bond is valued by discounting bond's cash flows at the yield level that is required by securities of comparable maturity, risk, liquidity and call features. Hence, the computation of a required yield level is a function of all of these factors
- The yield on a risky security can be represented by the yield on a comparable maturity risk-free security, plus a measure of the spread to Treasuries for default risk, plus a bond specific spread i.e.
- *Bond Yield = R_f + Spread to Treas. + Bond Specific Spread*

Bond Valuation and Interest Rates

14.5 Valuing a Bond:

- <u>Two important facts</u> associated with valuation and bond prices in the marketplace are:
- <u>Bond prices and changes in interest rates move in opposite directions</u>
- <u>Investors and traders value and bonds based on a price to worst call feature scenario</u>; i.e. issuer of the bond will act in its own best interest in calling or managing the bond's call features and will exercise the call at the first available opportunity that is economically advantageous to the issuer

Bond Valuation and Interest Rates

Valuing a Bond – Example:

- Let us value the bond of XYZ Inc. which has a face value of $1000, maturity of 10 years and pays interest semi-annually at a coupon rate of 8%
- We calculate the cash flows from the bond

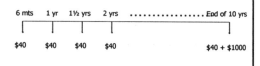

6 mts	1 yr	1½ yrs	2 yrs	. . . . End of 10 yrs
$40	$40	$40	$40	$40 + $1000

Bond Valuation and Interest Rates

Valuing a Bond – Discount Bond Example:

- If the interest rates for a 10-year bond of comparable risk were at 10%, we discount the 8% cash flows at 10% and calculate the present value of cash flows to find the bond value i.e. $875.38 in this case
- The market price of this bond is below or at a discount to its face value and is known as a discount bond
- Thus a discount bond has a coupon that is lower than the yield required by the market to sell a bond with comparable maturity, credit rating, and other features

---

Bond Valuation and Interest Rates

Valuing a Bond – Par Bond Example:

- Suppose the interest rates for a 10-year bond of comparable risk is 8% instead of 10%, we discount the cash flows at 8% and calculate the present value of cash flows which will give us a value of $1000 which is the face value of the bond
- A bond in which its coupon is equal to the yield required by the market to sell a bond with comparable maturity, credit rating, and other features will have a market price equal to its face value and is known as a Par Bond

Bond Valuation and Interest Rates

Valuing a Bond – Premium Bond Example:

- Suppose the interest rates for a 10-year, 8% coupon bond of comparable risk decreased to 7%, we discount the cash flows at 7% and calculate the present value of cash flows which will give us a value of $1071.06
- A bond in which its coupon is lower than the yield required by the market to sell a bond with comparable maturity, credit rating, and other features will have a market price higher than its face value and is known as a Premium Bond

Bond Valuation and Interest Rates

Using a Financial Calculator to Value a Bond:

- Take an example of a 10 year bond than pays interest semi annually at 10% and interest rates for a 10-year bond of similar risk is 9%, calculate the value of the bond
- We input values in the financial calculator:

  n = 20 (since payments are received semi annually)

  pmt = $50

  i = 4.5%

  fv = $1000

  Then solve for PV which is equal to $1065.04

Bond Valuation and Interest Rates

Valuing a Premium Bond to Call Date:

- Let us continue with the previous example and add that the bond is callable after 5 years at 101% of par value
- Since the bond is callable by the issuer we price it on the *price to worst* scenario, which usually assumes that the issuer will call the bond at the first available opportunity in which it makes economic sense
- Hence if the issuer calls the bond after 5 years at 101% of par value, the value of the bond is (inputting n=10, pmt=$50, i=4.5% & fv=1010 in the financial calculator and solving for PV) is $1046.00 and is lower than the value of non callable bond which was $1065.06.

Stock Valuation

Chapter 15:
Stock Valuation

Woolridge & Gray

How to Value a Stock

Chapter Objectives

- How to value a stock
- Discuss various approaches to stock valuation
- Discuss how to use the stock valuation program, ValuePro, and how to use the website Valuepro.net to value stocks

---

How to Value a Stock

Chapter Overview

- 15.1   Introduction to Stock Valuation
- 15.2   Return to Stockholders
- 15.3   Stock Valuation Approaches: Fundamental, Technical and MPT
- 15.4   The Discounted Free Cash Flow to the Firm Valuation Approach
- 15.5   Valuepro.net Online Stock Valuation Web Site

How to Value a Stock

15.1 Introduction to Stock Valuation

- Common stock represents a proportionate ownership interest in a corporation
- The value of a stock is crucially dependent upon the future profits or cash flows that the firm is expected to generate and the interest rate or required yield level that is expected from the investment
- Higher profits increase a stock's market value and lower profits decrease its value—a direct relationship
- Higher interest rates decrease market value and lower yields and interest rates increase value—an inverse relationship.

How to Value a Stock

15.1 Introduction to Stock Valuation

- A stock should be valued in the same manner as other financial asset—by discounting its expected cash flows at a risk-adjusted discounting rate.
- While valuing a stock it is important to remember that the range of future cash flows for a stock can be enormous. Cash flows can be higher or lower than expected, and we make some simplifying assumptions regarding the expected cash flows.
- A corporation is a legal entity that has an infinite life and the valuation procedure must address the issue of valuing cash flows to infinity.

How to Value a Stock

15.1 Introduction to Stock Valuation

- An asset that has a stream of even cash flows that continue to infinity is known as a perpetuity
- The value of a perpetuity is calculated by dividing the level annual cash flow associated with the perpetuity by the discounting rate:

Value of a Perpetuity = $\dfrac{\text{Annual Cash Flow}}{\text{Discounting Rate}}$

How to Value a Stock

15.2   Return to Stockholders

- Return to stockholders includes any dividend payments plus the increase (or minus the decrease) in stock price that investors experience during an investment holding period

% Return to Stockholders = $\frac{\text{(Dividends + Change in Stock Price)}}{\text{Beginning Stock Price}}$

- For example, if a stock's price started the year at $100, the stock paid $1 in dividends during the year, and it ended the year at $109, its percentage annual return to stockholders equals: ($1 + $9)/ $100 = 10%.

How to Value a Stock

Stock Value and Dividend Policy:

- The dividend policy of the firm should not affect the current value of a stock.
- However, the expected future value of a stock is greatly affected by dividend policy.
- When a company does not pay dividends and reinvests its earnings in projects, the investors receive no current dividend but instead receive an increase in stock price.

XYZ Dividend Company—Stock price stays constant—Investors receive 10% Dividend Return

	Table 15-1					
	XYZ Dividend Company-Stock Price Change					
	100% Dividend Payment					
	Market		Required		Net	Stock
Year	Equity	Earnings	Return	Dividend	Invest	Price
1	$1 billion	$100 million	10%	$100 million	0	$10
2	$1 billion	$100 million	10%	$100 million	0	$10
3	$1 billion	$100 million	10%	$100 million	0	$10

UVW Growth Company—Stock price increases 10% per year—Investors receive No Dividends

	Table 15-2					
	UVW Growth Company-Stock Price					
	0% Dividend Payment					
Year	Market Equity	Earnings	Required Return	Dividend	Net Invest	Stock Price
1	$1 billion	$100 million	10%	0	$100 million	10.00
2	$1.1 billion	$110 million	10%	0	$110 million	11.00
3	$1.21 billion	$121 million	10%	0	$121 million	12.10

How to Value a Stock

15.3 Stock Valuation Approaches

▪Professional stock market participants practice a number of investment approaches and techniques which is classified as fitting into one of three camps: Fundamental Analysis, Technical Analysis, and Modern Portfolio Theory (MPT)

▪ The three philosophies have different beliefs about the relationship between the stock prices that we observe in the markets and underlying intrinsic stock values

---

How to Value a Stock

Exhibit 15-1
Valuation Strategies

How to Value a Share?

	Technical Analysis	Fundamental Analysis	Portfolio Theory
What Drives Stock Prices?	Psychology Technical Cosmic	Earnings Dividends	Risk & Return
How to Value A Share?	Trends Waves Factors	Forecast Dividends & Earnings	Risk & Return
Relationship Between Value and Prices?	P ✗ V	P will Eventually Equal Value	P = V

How to Value a Stock

Technical Analysis

▪ Technical analysts believe that stock prices are influenced more by investor psychology and emotions of the crowd than by changes in the fundamentals of the company.

▪ Technical analysts chart historic stock price movements, volume of trading activity, and the price/volume aspects of related equity and debt markets to predict or anticipate the stock buying behavior of other market participants.

▪ Technical analysts generally have a shorter-term stock holding orientation and more frequent trading activity.

How to Value a Stock

Fundamental Analysis

▪ According to Fundamental Analysis approach, the company's current and future operating and financial performance determine the value of the company's stock

▪ The assumption underlying this approach is that a company's stock has a true or intrinsic value to which its price is anchored. When there is an price divergence, the price over time will gravitate to its intrinsic value.

▪ To assess a company's prospects, fundamental analysts evaluate overall economic, industry and company data to estimate a stock's value

How to Value a Stock

Fundamental Analysis – Target Stock Price

- Examples of fundamental analysis approach include DCF valuation, target stock price and relative valuation.
- Target Stock Price technique forecasts earnings per share (EPS) of a firm and multiplies EPS by the projected P/E ratio to arrive at a target stock price.
- Example: Suppose the projected EPS of XYZ Inc. is $2.50 and the market P/E ratio is 10. The target stock price of XYZ Inc. is $25. If the current market price of the stock is $20, a financial analyst would recommend buying the stock.

How to Value a Stock

Fundamental Analysis – Relative Valuation

- Relative value analysis employ measures of value such as P/E ratios, price/book values (P/BV), price/sales (P/S), or the price/earnings/growth (PEG) ratios for a company and compares them with those of similar stocks and industry peers
- Example: "McDonalds current P/E of 15.8 is below the P/Es of other fast food restaurant chains. Given that the company's growth in earnings and sales is in line with industry peers, and its risk profile is below that of its competitors, we conclude that McDonalds is undervalued"

How to Value a Stock

Fundamental Analysis – DCF Valuation

- In the DCF approach a stock's value is the sum of the expected cash flows of the company, discounted at an appropriate interest rate.
- The most basic DCF approach is the dividend discount model (DDM), under which an analyst estimates future dividend growth and the required rate of return on the stock and discounts those expected dividends to arrive at a stock's value.
- Other DCF approaches are the free cash flow to equity (FCFE) model and free cash flow to the firm (FCFF) model.

How to Value a Stock

Modern Portfolio Theory

- Efficient capital markets is a cornerstone of MPT and is the belief that stock prices always reflect intrinsic value, and that any type of fundamental or technical analysis is already embedded in the stock price.
- As such, MPT devotees tell investors not to bother to search for undervalued stocks but instead to pick a risk level that they can live with and diversify holdings among a portfolio of stocks.
- However empirical evidence shows that there is value to careful stock selection.

My Valuation Philosophy

There is value to careful stock selection (FA).

Timing of purchase and sale of stock is important (TA).

Diversification is good (MPT).

Value each stock holding individually and buy shares that are undervalued by (15)% and sell shares that are overvalued by (15)%

How to Value a Stock

Free Cash Flow to the Firm Valuation Approach

The discounted free cash flow to the firm valuation approach is a four-step process to value the stock of a company

Step 1: Forecast the company's Expected Cash Flow

Step 2: Estimate its Weighted Average Cost of Capital

Step 3: Calculate the Enterprise Value of the Company

Step 4: Calculate Intrinsic Stock Value

How to Value a Stock

Excess Return Period and Competitive Advantage

- The Excess Return Period is the period during which a company is able to earn returns on new investments that are greater than its cost of capital because of a competitive advantage enjoyed by the firm.

- Success attracts competitors and over time a company loses its competitive advantage and the return from its new investments just equals its WACC (i.e. investors are just compensated for the risk that they are taking in owning the company's stock and no additional value is created from new business investments).

How to Value a Stock

Excess Return Period and Competitive Advantage

Depending upon the excess return period companies can be grouped into 4 categories:

Boring companies - operate in a highly competitive, low-margin industry - a 1 year excess return period

Decent companies - decent reputation, don't control pricing or growth in their industry - a 5 year excess return period

Good companies - good brand names, large economies of scale - a 7 year excess return period

Great companies - great growth potential, tremendous marketing power, brand names - a 10 year excess return period

How to Value a Stock

Residual Value

- Once a company loses its competitive advantage the stock price of the company still grows in value, but its growth does not exceed its risk-adjusted market expectation of the investors.

- At that point in time, the after-tax earnings of the company can be treated and valued as what is known as a cash flow perpetuity—equal to the company's net operating profit after tax divided by its WACC. This discounted value is called the company's residual value.

- Residual value is very important—it generally represents 60% to 90% of the company's stock value.

How to Value a Stock

15.6 Valuepro.net Online Stock Valuation Web Site

- The Web site www.valuepro.net is devoted to the DCF method of stock valuation and has links that explain the approach in detail.
- Type a stock symbol into the slot on the home Web page, click on the Get Baseline Valuation button, and the online valuation program accesses data sources for information relating to the company that you are valuing and calculates twenty variables, puts them into a valuation algorithm and calculates the intrinsic stock value of the company using a simple discounted cash flow model.

How to Value a Stock

15.6 Valuepro.net Online Stock Valuation Web Site

How to Value a Stock

15.6 Valuepro.net Online Stock Valuation Web Site

- You can go to any or all of the input cells, put your own estimates into the cells, hit the Recalculate button, and the online valuation program calculates the new intrinsic stock value based on the inputs that you have provided

- If you want to see the detailed pro forma statement associated with the valuation, click on the Cash Flows button and a cash flow schedule based on the underlying inputs appears

Valuation of Microsoft

Use valuepro.net online valuation service to get general input page and cash flow page.

Look at price sensitivity to Growth Rate, NOPMs, and Interest Rates.

Stock Valuation Questions

How does the stock market come up with a stock's price?

Why do stock prices react so violently to small earnings surprises?

How do interest rate changes affect a stock's value?

How does the internet affect stock prices?

When should I sell a stock?

Focus of this Presentation

Explore how to value the common stock of most corporations:

using a small set of cash flow inputs

using a small set of cost of capital inputs

explore where to find the info that we need

introduce easy-to-use valuation software called ValuePro 2002

Overcome the fear of finance

Introduction to Stock Valuation

Definition of Valuation: the value **(current dollars, PV, hard cash) of** <u>any</u> **financial instrument (stock, bond, mortgage) equals the** present value **of its expected cash flows (think "real profits"),** discounted **(think "reduced") for** risk **and** timing.

Stock Valuation depends most on <u>profits</u> & <u>interest rates</u>.

Discounted Cash Flow: A Four Step Approach to Valuation

Step 1: Forecast Expected Cash Flows (think "real profits")

Step 2: Estimate the Discount Rate (think "interest rates")

Step 3: Calculate the Enterprise Value of the Corporation

Step 4: Calculate Per Share Stock Value

<u>Buy/Sell Decisions should be based solely on Price Versus Value!!!</u>

The best company is a poor investment if you pay too much!

Buy Decision: **If the stock's value is greater than a stock's price by (X)%, buy it.**

Sell Decision: **If the stock's value is less than a stock's price by (Y)%, sell it.**

Growth vs.Value, Large Cap vs. Small, Tech vs. non-Tech?

Should the classification of a stock affect it's value? NO!

Classification does affect *cash flow measures*- higher growth rates, larger NOPMs, higher required investment; and a company's *discount rate*- higher for the riskier cash flows

---

Stock Valuation Approaches

Fundamental Analysis
Technical Analysis
Modern Portfolio Theory

DCF is a Type of Fundamental Analysis

Assumption: a company's stock price will move towards its intrinsic value.

Many market players use FA as basis for long-term buy/sell decisions.

Investment Decision Rule: If Price < Value, buy; If Price > Value, sell.

Investor Expectations Regarding Stock Market Returns

S&P 500 50-year returns- 1946-96, S&P 500 7.13% real average yearly return vs. 6.96% EPS/price median earnings yield;

*Long term-***real stock returns (after inflation) closely track** *real growth in earnings***;**

Short term-interest rates **are most important influence on stock price.**

Is a Stock Fairly Valued?

How are market *expectations* factored into a stock's price?

What happens when performance equals expectations? Microsoft

What happens when performance exceeds expectations? WLA, AMEX

What happens when performance is less than expectations? Computer Associates

Stock Value Versus Stock Price

The effect of News on Stock Prices- Entremed

Does the stock market ever over react or under react to new information?

Do emotions often play a large role in the stock market?

Why don't brokers recommend selling a stock?

Where to Get Info for Valuation?

Two principal sources on Internet:

The best source for cash flow inputs is the investor relations link of the company's own Web site- annual audit and earnings and press releases. Info on revenue, NOPM, investment rate, working capital, historic growth.

Yahoo! Finance, or MSN Money. Gives stock price, beta, shares outstanding, projected growth rates, interest rates.

Key Statistics for Microsoft-Yahoo Finance

Microsoft's Stock Price: A Mature Growth Company

4/18/2004 price of $25.16/share, 10.79Bil shares

Total Market Cap- $271.5 Billion

8.4 times sales of $32.19 Billion, P/E is 30.83

Pays $.16 annual dividend (0.64%) and actively repurchases shares

Beta = 1.585 Yahoo, Anal. Growth rate=10%

Analyst recommendations- Strong Buy-16, Buy-16, Hold-3, Sell-0, Strong Sell-0

Microsoft 2003 Income Statement

Income Statement		Get Income Statement for:		GO
View: Quarterly Data | Annual Data				All numbers in thousands
PERIOD ENDING		30-Jun-03	30-Jun-02	30-Jun-01
Total Revenue		32,187,000	28,365,000	25,296,000
Cost of Revenue		5,686,000	5,191,000	3,455,000
Gross Profit		26,501,000	23,174,000	21,841,000
Operating Expenses				
Research Development		4,659,000	4,307,000	4,379,000
Selling General and Administrative		8,625,000	6,957,000	5,742,000
Non Recurring		-	-	-
Others		-	-	-
Total Operating Expenses		-	-	-
Operating Income or Loss		13,217,000	11,910,000	11,720,000
Income from Continuing Operations				
Total Other Income/Expenses Net		1,509,000	(397,000)	(195,000)
Earnings Before Interest And Taxes		14,726,000	11,513,000	11,525,000
Interest Expense		-	-	-
Income Before Tax		14,726,000	11,513,000	11,525,000
Income Tax Expense		4,733,000	3,684,000	3,804,000
Minority Interest		-	-	-
Net Income From Continuing Ops		9,993,000	7,829,000	7,721,000
Non-recurring Events				
Discontinued Operations		-	-	-
Extraordinary Items		-	-	-
Effect Of Accounting Changes		-	-	(375,000)
Other Items		-	-	-
Net Income		9,993,000	7,829,000	7,346,000
Preferred Stock And Other Adjustments		-	-	-
Net Income Applicable To Common Shares		$9,993,000	$7,829,000	$7,346,000

Microsoft NOPM Calculation

			Microsoft			
			3-YEAR NOPM HISTORY			
			(in millions of dollars)			
Year	Revenue	CGS	SG&A	R&D	NOP	NOPM
2003	32,187	5,686	8,625	4,659	13,217	41.06%
2002	28,365	5,191	6,957	4,307	11,910	41.99%
2001	25,296	3,455	5,742	4,379	11,720	46.33%
3-Year Average						43.13%

Microsoft 2003 Balance Sheet

Balance Sheet	Get Balance Sheet for:		GO
View: Quarterly Data | Annual Data			All numbers in thousands
PERIOD ENDING	30-Jun-03	30-Jun-02	30-Jun-01
Assets			
Current Assets			
Cash And Cash Equivalents	6,438,000	1,114,000	3,922,000
Short Term Investments	42,610,000	37,538,000	27,678,000
Net Receivables	7,702,000	7,241,000	5,620,000
Inventory	640,000	673,000	-
Other Current Assets	1,583,000	2,010,000	2,417,000
Total Current Assets	58,973,000	48,576,000	39,637,000
Long Term Investments	13,692,000	14,191,000	14,141,000
Property Plant and Equipment	2,223,000	2,268,000	2,309,000
Goodwill	3,128,000	1,426,000	-
Intangible Assets	384,000	243,000	-
Accumulated Amortization	-	-	-
Other Assets	1,171,000	942,000	3,170,000
Deferred Long Term Asset Charges	-	-	-
Total Assets	79,571,000	67,646,000	59,257,000
Liabilities			
Current Liabilities			
Accounts Payable	13,974,000	12,744,000	11,132,000
Short/Current Long Term Debt	5,033,000	4,375,000	3,398,000
Other Current Liabilities	8,941,000	8,369,000	7,734,000
Total Current Liabilities	13,974,000	12,744,000	11,132,000
Long Term Debt	-	-	-
Other Liabilities	2,846,000	2,324,000	-
Deferred Long Term Liability Charges	1,731,000	398,000	836,000
Minority Interest	-	-	-
Negative Goodwill	-	-	-
Other Assets	1,171,000	942,000	3,170,000
Deferred Long Term Asset Charges	-	-	-
Total Liabilities	18,551,000	15,466,000	11,968,000

Microsoft Working Capital Calcualtion

	Microsoft					
	2-YEAR WORKING CAPITAL HISTORY					
	(in millions of dollars)					
Year	Revenue	Acct. Rec.	Inventory	Acct. Pay.	Working Cap	% Work. Cap.
2003	$32,187	$7,702	$640	$5,033	$3,309	10.28%
2002	$28,365	$7,241	$673	$8,941	-$1,027	-3.62%
2-year average						3.33%

Microsoft 2003 Cash Flow Statement

Cash Flow   Get Cash Flow for: [ ] GO

View: Quarterly Data | **Annual Data**   All numbers in thousands

PERIOD ENDING	30-Jun-03	30-Jun-02	30-Jun-01
Net Income	9,993,000	7,829,000	7,346,000
Operating Activities, Cash Flows Provided By or Used In			
Depreciation	1,439,000	1,084,000	1,536,000
Adjustments To Net Income	3,319,000	4,020,000	4,843,000
Changes In Accounts Receivables	187,000	(1,623,000)	(418,000)
Changes In Liabilities	475,000	1,865,000	927,000
Changes In Inventories	-	-	-
Changes In Other Operating Activities	384,000	1,534,000	(812,000)
Total Cash Flow From Operating Activities	15,797,000	14,509,000	13,422,000
Investing Activities, Cash Flows Provided By or Used In			
Capital Expenditures	(891,000)	(770,000)	(1,103,000)
Investments	(5,259,000)	(10,075,000)	(7,631,000)
Other Cashflows from Investing Activities	(1,063,000)	-	-
Total Cash Flows From Investing Activities	(7,213,000)	(10,845,000)	(8,734,000)
Financing Activities, Cash Flows Provided By or Used In			
Dividends Paid	(857,000)	-	-
Sale Purchase of Stock	(4,366,000)	(4,572,000)	(5,821,000)
Net Borrowings	-	-	-
Other Cash Flows from Financing Activities	-	-	235,000
Total Cash Flows From Financing Activities	(5,223,000)	(4,572,000)	(5,586,000)
Effect Of Exchange Rate Changes	61,000	2,000	(26,000)
Change In Cash and Cash Equivalents	$3,422,000	($906,000)	($924,000)

Microsoft Investment and Depreciation Calculation

	MICROSOFT					
	3-YEAR INVESTMENT AND DEPRECIATION HISTORY					
	(in millions of dollars)					
Year	Revenue	Investment	% Investment	Depreciation	% Depreciation	Net Investment
2003	$32,187	$891	2.77%	$1,439	4.47%	-$548
2002	$28,365	$770	2.71%	$1,084	3.82%	-$314
2001	$25,296	$1,103	4.36%	$1,536	6.07%	-$433
3-year average			3.28%		4.79%	

Microsoft DCF Valuation

Step 1: Forecast Microsoft's expected cash flow

Step 2: Estimate Microsoft's discount rate

Step 3: Calculate the Enterprise value of Microsoft

Step 4: Calculate Microsoft's per share stock value

Step 1: Forecast Expected Cash Flow

We use the DCF free cash flow to firm to value Microsoft's stock;

Free cash flows are cash amounts that are available to be paid to stockholders;

Activities that produce net cash *inflows* to firm have *positive* effect on stock value;

Activities that produce net cash *outflows* from firm have *negative* effect on value.

Free Cash Flow to Firm

FCFF = Revenues - operating expenses - net investment (fixed and working capital) - taxes;

To calculate FCFF, we need five important cash flow measures that we call *The Five Chinese Brothers*

The Five Chinese Brothers
Microsoft-Baseline Valuation

Revenue Growth Rate: historical is 8.7%, analyst expected 5-year growth rate is <u>10</u>%;

NOPM – 2001-03= <u>43.13</u>%

Tax Rate- 2001-03= <u>33</u>%

Investment- 2001-03= <u>3.28</u>%

Depreciation- 2001-03= <u>4.79</u>%

Incremental Working Capital= <u>3.33</u>%

Microsoft: Cost of Capital Inputs

Market Stock Price= $<u>25.16</u>

Beta estimate (Yahoo)= <u>1.585</u>

Risk-Free 10-year rate= <u>4.35</u>%

Shares Outstanding= <u>10.79</u> Billion

Total Current Assets= $<u>58,973</u>

Total Current Liabilities= $<u>13,974</u>

ValuePro 2002 - [VP2002.BWB]
File Edit ValuePro Window Help

Valuation Date   04/18/2004

ValuePro 2002
General Input Screen
Intrinsic Stock Value $23.64
General Inputs

Company Ticker....	MSFT		
Excess Return Period (years)	10	Depreciation Rate (% of Rev.)	4.79
Revenues ($mil)	32187	Investment Rate (% of Rev.)	3.28
Growth Rate (%)	10.00	Working Capital (% of Rev.)	3.33
Net Operating Profit Margin (%)	43.13	Short-Term Assets ($mil)	58973
Tax Rate (%)	33.00	Short-Term Liabilities($mil)	13974
Stock Price($)	25.16	Equity Risk Premium (%)	3.00
Shares Outstanding (mil)	10879	Company Beta	1.58
10-year Treasury Yield (%)	4.35	Value of Debt Out. ($mil)	0
Bond Spread to Treasury (%)	0.00	Value of Pref. Stock Out. ($mil)	0
Preferred Stock Yield (%)	0.00	Company WACC (%)	9.18

WACC-Expected Return for a Stock

Returns for an individual stock should depend on *risk* of the stock

With increasing risk, investors should demand higher expected returns;

How is risk measured? Beta!

How is expected return measured? CAPM!

Expected Return from a Stock= Risk Free Rate + Beta*(Equity Risk Premium)

Estimate Microsoft's Discounting Rate--Its WACC

Assume the following:

Microsoft has no debt or preferred stock outstanding

Risk-free 10 Treasury rate = 4.35%

Equity Risk Premium = 3%

Microsoft's beta = 1.585

Therefore Microsoft's WACC = 9.10%

ValuePro 2002 - [VP2002.BWB]

File Edit ValuePro Window Help

Valuation Date 04/18/2004

ValuePro 2002
Weighted Average Cost of Capital Screen
MSFT

Cost of Common Equity

10-Year Treasury Bond Yield	4.35
Company Specific Beta	1.58
Equity Risk Premium	3.00
Cost of Common Equity	9.10

Market Capitalization and After-Tax Weighted Average Cost of Capital

	Current Yield	After Tax Yield	Market Value	% Capitalization	Weighted After-Tax Yield
Long-Term Debt	4.35	2.91	$0	0.0%	0.00
Preferred Stock	0.00	0.00	$0	0.0%	0.00
Common Stock	9.10	9.10	$273,716	100.0%	9.10
			$273,716	100.0%	9.10

Step 4: Calculate Microsoft's Per Share Stock Value- $23.64

Start with total corporate value: $271.201 billion

Subtract value of debt + preferred stock + short-term liabilities: $13.974 billion

Divide the difference-$257.227 (Total Value to Common Equity) by shares outstanding: 10.79 billion;

Result = $23.64 Intrinsic Stock Value

ValuePro 2002 - [VP2002.fIwB]

File   Edit   ValuePro   Window   Help

Valuation Date   04/16/2004

ValuePro 2002
General Pro Forma Screen
10-year Excess Return Period
MSFT

Disc. Excess Return Period FCFF		$101,378		Total Corporate Value			$271,201					
Discounted Residual Value		$110,950		Less Debt			$0					
Short-Term Assets		$58,573.0		Less Preferred Stock			$0					
Total Corporate Value		$271,201		Less Short-Term Liabilities			($13,974)					
				Total Value to Common Equity			$257,227					
				Intrinsic Stock Value			$23.64					

(2)	(3)	(4)	(5)	(6)	(7)	(8)	(9)	(10)	(11)	(12)	(13)
12 Months Ending	Revenues	NOP	Adj. Taxes	NOPAT	Invest.	Deprec.	Change in Invest.	Change in Working Capital	FCFF	Discount Factor	Discounted FCFF
04/18/2004	32,187										
04/18/2005	35,406	15,270	5,039	10,231	1,161	1,696	-535	107	10,659	0.9165	9,769
04/18/2006	38,946	16,798	5,543	11,254	1,277	1,866	-588	118	11,725	0.8401	9,849
04/18/2007	42,841	18,477	6,098	12,380	1,405	2,052	-647	130	12,897	0.7700	9,930
04/18/2008	47,125	20,325	6,707	13,618	1,546	2,257	-712	143	14,187	0.7057	10,012
04/18/2009	51,837	22,368	7,378	14,980	1,700	2,483	-783	157	15,605	0.6468	10,094
04/18/2010	57,021	24,593	8,116	16,477	1,870	2,731	-861	173	17,166	0.5928	10,176
04/18/2011	62,723	27,053	8,927	18,125	2,057	3,004	-947	190	18,882	0.5434	10,260
04/18/2012	68,996	29,758	9,820	19,938	2,263	3,305	-1,042	209	20,771	0.4980	10,344
04/18/2013	75,895	32,734	10,802	21,932	2,489	3,635	-1,146	230	22,848	0.4565	10,429
04/18/2014	83,485	36,007	11,882	24,125	2,738	3,999	-1,261	253	25,133	0.4184	10,515
	83,485	36,007	11,882	24,125	3,999	3,999	0	0	264,961	0.4184	110,950

Stock Valuation Questions
Is Microsoft really worth $271.59 Billion?

How does the stock market come up with a stock's price?

Why do stock prices react so violently to small earnings surprises?

How do interest rate changes affect a stock's value?

When should I sell a stock?

Managing Risk: Diversifying, Hedging, Insuring, and Derivative Securities

Chapter 16: Management of Risk—Diversifying, Hedging, Insuring and Derivative Securities

Woolridge & Gray

Management of Risk: Diversifying, Hedging, Insuring and Derivative Securities

Chapter objectives

The risk of financial assets and how that risk can be managed;

The process of diversification;

Hedging and how it can be done effectively;

Derivative securities and how they may be used to reduce risk.

Management of Risk: Diversifying, Hedging, Insuring and Derivative Securities

Chapter overview

16.1 The management of risk

16.2 Diversification– the costless way to reduce risk

16.3 Hedging– sacrifice gain to protect against loss

16.4 Insurance– pay a premium to protect against loss

16.5 Derivative securities

Management of Risk: Diversifying, Hedging, Insuring and Derivative Securities

16.1 The management of risk

Risk is usually measured by the volatility of the rate of return, such as standard deviation

Trade off between risk and return:
The higher the return, the higher the risk

	Ibbotson & Sinquefield Study		
Asset Class	**Compound Annual Return**	**Simple Average Annual Return**	**Std. Dev. of Return**
U.S. Treasury Bills	3.80%	3.90%	3.20%
U.S. Treasury Bonds	5.30%	5.70%	9.40%
Corporate Bonds	5.80%	6.10%	8.60%
Large Company Stocks	10.70%	12.70%	20.20%
Small Company Stocks	12.50%	17.30%	33.20%

Management of Risk: Diversifying, Hedging, Insuring and Derivative Securities

16.1 The management of risk

Investors are usually risk averse

Ways to reduce risk associated with financial assets

Diversification
  Spread the risk by investing in a number of risky assets

Hedging
  By using techniques to lock-in a price or return

Insurance
  Pay a premium to purchase a contract to protect

Sell the assets

Management of Risk: Diversifying, Hedging, Insuring and Derivative Securities

16.2 Diversification– the costless way to reduce risk

As long as the returns of assets are not perfectly correlated, diversification acts to reduce risk

Correlation

Measures the degree to which the movement of variables are related, and can range between -1.0 to 1.0

Correlation of 1.0 means when one stock up 10%, the other stock also up 10%

Correlation of -1.0 means when one stock up 10%, the other stock down 10%

Assets that are highly correlated offer less risk reduction

Management of Risk: Diversifying, Hedging, Insuring and Derivative Securities

16.2 Diversification– the costless way to reduce risk

Stockholders face two types of risk: systematic risk and unsystematic risk

Total Risk = Systematic Risk + Unsystematic Risk

Systematic risk

Represents the risk of the stock market

It is caused by economy, taxes, and other market factors

It can not be diversified away

Unsystematic risk

Is specific to a company

Diversification reduces the unsystematic risk

Management of Risk: Diversifying, Hedging, Insuring and Derivative Securities

16.2 Diversification– the costless way to reduce risk

Diversification is easy to obtain in a portfolio

Achieving the highest return for certain level of risk is known as investing on the efficient frontier

Studies show that 20—25 stocks are sufficient to reduce risk

Number of Stocks in Portfolio	Average Standard Deviation of Annual Portfolio Returns	Ratio of Portfolio Standard Deviation of a Single Stock
1	49.24%	100%
10	23.93%	49%
50	20.20%	41%
100	19.69%	40%
300	19.34%	39%
500	19.27%	39%
1000	19.21%	39%

Management of Risk: Diversifying, Hedging, Insuring and Derivative Securities

16.3 Hedging – sacrifice gain to protect against loss

There are three types of hedging instruments

Future contracts

A forward contract with standardized terms that trades on an organized exchange

Forward contracts

A written agreement between two parties that is not traded on an organized exchange

Swaps

An agreement between two or more parties to exchange sets of cash flows over a period of time

Interest swap and currency swap

Management of Risk: Diversifying, Hedging, Insuring and Derivative Securities

16.3 Hedging – sacrifice gain to protect against loss

Some terms relating to hedging

Hedgers and speculators

Long position and short position

Value and size of a contract

Spot price and forward price

When an investor hedges, he fixes the sales price for the asset and gives up any upside gain for offloading the risk of loss.

Management of Risk: Diversifying, Hedging, Insuring and Derivative Securities

16.4 Insurance– pay a premium to protect against loss

Insurance contracts

Cap-Limitation of the amount of money paid under a claim

Deductibles

Option

Financial assets that have characteristics similar to insurance contracts

Represents the right to sell or purchase an asset at a fixed price at a fixed time in the future

---

Management of Risk: Diversifying, Hedging, Insuring and Derivative Securities

16.4 Insurance– pay a premium to protect against loss

Option

Strike price

Also known as exercise price, predetermined

Expiration date

After which the option can no longer be exercised

Call option

Call option contracts enable the owner to buy an asset

Put option

Put option contracts enables the owner to sell an asset

Management of Risk: Diversifying, Hedging, Insuring and Derivative Securities

16.4 Insurance– pay a premium to protect against loss

Option

S = current market price of security underlying the option

Xc = exercise price or strike price on the call option

Xp = exercise price or strike price on the put option

The call option is in the money if $S > Xc$

The put option is in the money if $S < Xp$

An option has positive value to its owner before expiration

The price or value of a call or put option has two components:

Intrinsic value and Time value

Management of Risk: Diversifying, Hedging, Insuring and Derivative Securities

16.4 Insurance– pay a premium to protect against loss

Value of Option

Intrinsic value

The amount the option is in the money and is the difference between the current price and the strike price of the option.

Time value

Reflects expectations of an option's profitability associated with exercising it at some future point in time

---

Management of Risk: Diversifying, Hedging, Insuring and Derivative Securities

16.4 Insurance– pay a premium to protect against loss

Value of Option

Example

If McDonald's stock is trading at $20 per share and the strike price of an option that expires in six months is $18, and the option is trading at a price of $3.80, the intrinsic value of the option is:

Intrinsic Value = $S - Xc$ = $20 - $18 = $2

Time Value of Option = $3.80 - $2 = $1.80

Management of Risk: Diversifying, Hedging, Insuring and Derivative Securities

16.5 Derivative securities

Derivative securities

Financial instruments

Value derived from or is based on

    The value of a simple security or

    The level of an interest rate or

    Interest rate index or

    Stock market index

Delivery occurs sometimes many years into the future, and buyer or seller can offset transactions

---

Management of Risk: Diversifying, Hedging, Insuring and Derivative Securities

16.5 Derivative securities

Derivative securities

Many securities have features embedded in them that make them derivative securities, such as callable bonds, and convertible bonds

Value Call Option = Value Callable Bond – Value Non-Callable Bond

Derivative securities often are more sensitive to price or yield changes, and sometimes are more leveraged

    Attractive to hedgers

    Can backfire for speculators

Management of Risk: Diversifying, Hedging, Insuring and Derivative Securities

16.5 Derivative securities

Derivative securities

Example

    Let's assume that the 30-year bond that is callable in 10 years issued by ABC Company is trading at 100% and has an 8% coupon. Let's also assume that the yield for a non-callable 30-year bond of a company with default risk similar to ABC Company is 7%.

What's the value of the call option?

Management of Risk: Diversifying, Hedging, Insuring and Derivative Securities

16.5 Derivative securities

Derivative securities

Answer to the example

Step 1 Non-callable bond present value
   PV = $1124.72
   (Using Excel or calculator n=60, PMT=40, i=3.5 FV=1000)

Step 2 The value of callable bond $1000

Step 3 Value of the call option is
   1000- 1124.72 = -$124.72

Management of Risk: Diversifying, Hedging, Insuring and Derivative Securities

16.5 Derivative securities

Types of derivative securities

Equity and Debt Components:
   Embedded with the characteristics of a simple stock or bond.
   The bond component can be fixed-rate, zero-coupon, or amortizing.

Option or price insurance components:
   Interest rate floors and caps, call and put options.
   Zero or positive values are associated with these components for the *owner* of the option.
   Zero or negative values are associated with these components for the *writer* of the option.

Management of Risk: Diversifying, Hedging, Insuring and Derivative Securities

16.5 Derivative securities

Types of derivative securities

Hedging or price-fixing components:
   Forward, futures contracts, interest rate and currency swap

   The value of these components may be positive or negative, depending on movements and shifts in yields, currency levels, or spot prices.

   The relative value at the time of issuance of the derivative security is zero.

   Generally have little upfront cost and are the most efficient type of hedging contract.

Management of Risk: Diversifying, Hedging, Insuring and Derivative Securities

16.5 Derivative securities

Relationship between cash and derivative markets

Prices of assets are related
Costs of storage and delivery are associated with futures and forwards

The concept of arbitrage and the law of one price
Investors constantly check the cash and derivative market to look for arbitrage opportunities

The law of one price dictates that the futures price of an asset and the spot price of the asset must be the same on the day future contracts expire

---

Management of Risk: Diversifying, Hedging, Insuring and Derivative Securities

16.5 Derivative securities

Valuation of derivative securities

The value depends upon the value of the underlying simple securities or building blocks

The value is usually based on following inputs:
The spot price and movement of the underlying assets
The amount of time to the expiration or delivery date
The exercise price
The risk free rate of interest
For option, the volatility associated with the underlying assets

---

Management of Risk: Diversifying, Hedging, Insuring and Derivative Securities

16.5 Derivative securities

Role of derivative markets

More liquid than spot markets
Transaction cost is lower
Less capital is required

More efficient than spot market
Encourage arbitrageurs to participate and drive price to equilibrium
Invoke the law of one price and does not allow arbitrage opportunities to exist for a long time

Can be used to manage risk or to speculate

Management of Risk: Diversifying, Hedging, Insuring and Derivative Securities

Summary

Management of risk
  Risk associated with the returns of financial assets
  Diversification, hedging and insurance to reduce risk

Diversification
  Reduce risk by investing on not highly correlated assets
  Reduce unsystematic risk
  Costless way to reduce risk

Hedging
  Reduce risk by sacrificing upside gain
  Future, forward and swap

Insurance
  Reduce risk by paying a premium. Option is similar to insurance
  The intrinsic value of an option is the difference between the exercise price and
    current price

Derivative securities
  The value is based on underlying simple securities
  The market is more efficient, liquid and used to hedge risk